Memories

—Of my wife, Debi Cordero—

04/07/1952 - 06/09/2022

By George Cordero

Published by
GRAPH Publishing, L.L.C.
www.graphpublishing.com

Printed in the U.S.A.

Introduction

Although there is no possible way to put down the combined memories of the fifty-five years of my life spent with this wonderful woman, my wife, friend, companion and lover. I'm hoping reading this will spark the memories her Children, Grandchildren and Great Grandchildren cherished about her in their lives.

I dedicate this small effort on my part to our Children, Grandchildren, Great Grandchildren and of those whose lives she touched.

-Her Loving Husband George

My Dearest Debi

I know I've probably told you about many of these feelings and the things we went through, but I want to write it down for your memory book.

We had fifty-five years together, fifty-five years raising our Children, Grandchildren and Great Grandchildren, you giving me and them a home and loving us, fifty-five years surviving all the heartbreaks and loss, together finding the strength to go on, fifty-five years holding tightly to each other. I now face the world without you. I know the huge hole I feel in my chest will never close as I know my heart will never be whole again. In whatever time I have left, I will continue to tell you "I love you" each day until we are together again. I love you, Debi.

I got orders to Hill AFB Utah from tech school and after four years I was given orders to Vietnam. After a year's tour of duty I was assigned to Sheppard AFB Texas.

I got orders to Sheppard AFB Texas. I came home from Vietnam an alcoholic with a lot of head problems. I was a player and just out for fun, that's all I was interested in. Nothing much else mattered. Those were my basic days, work, drink and play. One day I pulled into "P three" (Pioneer Three) a local drive-in that sold beer, burgers and other fast food. One of my normal hangouts. They had cute car hops. I noticed you walking across the lot with a tray of food and drinks thinking to myself "Damn where did she come from?" You were stunning, so damn cute. I thought to myself "I need to get to know her." So next time I came in, I made sure to park in your section of the lot. You came over and asked me what I wanted so I said a date? You gave me the "look" (something I would get to know well through the years) you said politely "I only serve food and drinks." That didn't go well. So, I ordered a beer and a burger. You brought it and walked away without a word. Course now I had a challenge. I wasn't used to this. Over the next few months, I did get you to stop and just talk while I flirted. After a bit we talked without flirting because all I'd get was "The Look" and you would walk away. Oh, I did still try but you always found a way to hand me my ass on a platter. One example was a trip Ken (a friend of mine and yours later) and I took a trip to Amarillo for an all-girls college frat party. Ken asked to borrow my car for a bit, so I said sure. He came back a couple of hours later and after a while we headed home. It had been raining that night, so the car was dirty. I dropped him off then went to "P three" to get a bite to eat and of course parked in your section. Told you I'd gone to a party and had thought of you. I noticed you were not looking at me but the back seat of the car. I turned and saw a bra lying on the seat! I just slumped down in the seat thinking what the hell! Who leaves a bra in a car? You casually ran your hand on the car door and then wiped your hand on my white shirt saying, "You need to wash your car George" and walked away. Another carhop came out to serve me. I began to realize this girl is not into games, up front and serious with a sense of humor. I really liked that. I was bringing a couple of the car hops to work each morning (we all partied at night) and I was starting to look at you in a whole different light and really did want to know you better. I thought if you were going to give me the time of day right now you sure weren't interested. Sort of untouchable. I worried that maybe you really didn't like me. (I was kind of a self-centered butt and knew that) you needed to see me in a better light? I decided to drop out of the "party nights" for a while. I was sitting in the parking lot pondering on how to safely ask you out on a date, my chance came sort of. Your shift was over early, and you came over to my car and asked if I'd give you a ride home, "straight home" saying it like maybe I'd kidnap you or something!! Of course, I said yes, and it turned out you lived on base with your sister and her husband. Your sister Roseanne invited me in, and we talked a bit. I asked you if you would help me wash my car (I had a sixty-seven red convertible chevy super sport) and I'd get you a coke and burger for helping. You looked at your sister with a "I don't know look" and she said, "go on". So, we washed the car and talked a lot for real then went to "P three" you only wanted a coke. After a while I was about to ask you out on a date, but before I could, You said, OOPS! I have to go my dates here! You got out of my car and got in some other guy's car and left. I Felt like John Travolta stranded at the drive-in from Grease. Well, figured that was that! Now my pride was hurt, and I was done trying with you. Next day there I was again in your section at "P three" of course. You came over and apologized and said you had forgotten he was meeting you there. (So as not to boost my ego 5 years later you told me he took you home early because your mind was not on him "but the other guy"). So, seeing my chance, I asked you out for Saturday, your day off, you said yes but wanted to cruise the Vard (no drive-in like I'd planned). We had a great time, and we talked and laughed a lot. After that, we dated more (sort of off and on) just driving and hanging out. Thinking back, I feel you just wanted to make me try harder. The more we dated the more I was just getting into you, having feelings for you. I'd pick you up from work and we would meet up with friends, cruise and go to a couple of parties. You really didn't care for the wilder group, so we mostly just hung out, I liked showing you off.

You remember our real date? I made reservations at a really nice restaurant. You were wearing a pleated white skirt, powder blue short sleeve shirt with collar that just made your eyes stand out. Damn but you were so hot! I wore a dress shirt and slacks. Note to self-here's your chance to show her you have class and are suave' in a public place. Well Mr. Class and suave' in the middle of dinner, I pick up a corner of the tablecloth and wipe my mouth. I just go blank and look up at you, I'm sure I looked like a deer in headlights. You had your head down, hand on your brow saying, "What are you doing?" In a last-ditch effort to save whatever "suave "I had left, I said "what? I'm using silverware" you laughed, and I felt like I just missed the bullet. To this day I don't know what made me do something that stupid. I do know that around you I just did stupid things I guess trying so hard to impress you. Before each date I'd have butterflies in my stomach, I know that it's probably a "girly" thing, but you had me so emotionally tied to everything about you. I was in love with you. You complained that your tips had dropped off quite a bit since you started really dating me. We both knew a lot of people and of course the guys knew you were off the market. You asked me to cut back on my drinking when we went out. Surprisingly it was not hard to stop drinking and my driving with you in the car, not a good idea, so yea, I really did. You where an inexpensive date never took much to please you, but boy you could drink, or so I thought. Until you finally asked me for a coke one day saying, "I didn't like beer". I asked where all the beer had gone, and you gave me this sheepish grin saying "Out the door". More reason to stop. Oh, but I loved that sheepish grin and your sweet smile in general.

As the months went on, we spent more time with your sister and brother-in-law with dinners as I got to know them better. After all those dates one day your sister asked you to tell me the color of my eyes since she had asked you and you'd said brown? Wow! I got eyeball to eyeball with you and asked again. Oh! You said, green!! One evening at the dinner table your sister Roseanne asked if you had told me? I was a bit confused; you took a deep breath, turned your chair to face me and said, "I'm sixteen". I was stunned! First you sure didn't look 16, and you had such maturity and grace that it never occurred to me to ask. Second, I was twenty-one and, in those days, I was looking at 20 years in jail! And we had dated for over eight months, so you were 15 when we met! You just smiled, Giggled and said, "I guess you have to marry me now huh" (It had been on my mind to ask, and this was the first time it had been mentioned. I had already planned the ring and knee and all that). So yes, I asked you to marry me! The smart ass you are said "let me think about it". I blurted out "you have to marry me I've told my commander!" Just another time you managed to get me so flustered I didn't know what I was saying (I was twenty-one, I didn't need my commander's permission) You giggled and said "yes". Doug and your sister Roseanne were all for it and excited. So was I, and there you sat tears falling down your cheek, God but you had my heart.

We went to see your mom a couple of weeks later and you blessed me with your hand in marriage in a little chapel in Waukegan, Illinois on November the 13th 1969. Now you were really mine and I loved you so much Debi. Thinking back, if not for you honey, I'd have been a homeless drunk or dead, I was on a path to nowhere. You put such peace and strength in me. I would do anything in the world for you. You loved me more than I loved myself and saw more in me than I knew I had. Your smile, tenderness, humor, the warmth of the love that you gave so freely. You honestly made me a better person beyond what I would have ever been alone. You kept my head straight and were always there to hold me when it was bad; you gave me the strength to control it (PTSD). You showed me what real love is. Your love for me made me feel powerful and gave me purpose in my life. We moved into a small house in Wichita Falls. Our first baby Missy was born and even though, I had been married before with two children. (She divorced me while I was in Vietnam) I had never seen anyone be the perfect first-time mother like you. You cared for her like you had been doing it all your life. The changing table you set up had baby wipes powder, soap and diapers always ready. I'd pick her up after work and she always smelled so good of lotion, powder and squeaky clean our life was perfect.

Remember the first and only time you ever slapped me? I do! I came home, and you were in the backyard hanging up clothes with the crib by the back door. I picked up Missy and went to the living room in the front of the house and sat down to play with her. You came in hysterical and in a panic, slapped me hard across the face and grabbed Missy then sat down crying and hugging her. Through your tears you yelled at me "Don't you ever do that to me again!" From that point on I always let you know I was home. Damn! The mark from your hand stayed all day. You didn't apologize but later kissed me on the cheek. You always worried so much about your children up through your grandchildren and great grandchildren.

We took Missy everywhere with us, always ready to show her off to our friends and cruising the Vard. She was such a pretty and happy baby. Spent a lot of time with good friends and our quiet time at home. Your favorite time was at home with your baby and me. I remember I was painting the house and came home with you coming to me at the door with a hug and kiss saying "It wasn't her fault" and you showed me my military overcoat covered in paint. Of course, I didn't get mad about it, just threw it away. Years later you confessed you had been the one to spill the paint on my coat but knew I wouldn't get mad at the baby. Sneaky of you huh? I wouldn't have gotten angry at you Debi, it was just a coat. We would have time out (babysitter) and go to the club dancing, if it was country "Little Ray" a close friend of ours would come and steal you to line dance, damn if you two didn't look great together. Yep, note to George you need to learn.

We received orders to Charleston AFB South Carolina. We bought a house and had our second child, Glen. Your water broke and you still wanted to shop for boys' clothes and I'm asking you "How do you know it's a boy?" (at that time we didn't know the sex of our children) your comment was "The way I'm carrying him." So, I'm thinking where does she come up with this stuff? In later years, I came to learn how perceptive you were and trusting of your feelings was amazing. I was a nervous wreck and finally drove you to the hospital against your wishes and waited a few more hours for him to come. Of course, it was a boy. I (of course) had to show him off like with Missy all over town.

Disaster struck us when he contracted spinal meningitis at three years of age. We nearly lost him, and you were so very defeated and hurt wanting me to fix it, as it seems you felt I could fix anything. He was in intensive care for over two weeks at the Naval Station Hospital. We were there every day, and we were told we must wait and see how he would do. Once a nurse told us we had to leave because visiting hours were over, and they had no facilities for us. I told her she would need help to get us to leave because all we needed were the two chairs we were sitting on. We didn't see her again.

Finally, we were told he was out of danger and was soon transferred to the ward. The nurses would take him from his crib and play with him again, a happy baby. He survived but was left deaf and had a slight paralysis on his left side. We didn't know anything about raising a deaf child or anything about paralysis. We sued the doctor and won Glen some money after five years. Because twice we were sent home to manage a cold and if the doctor would have done a spinal tap since he had all the symptoms of meningitis. He could have been treated early and been fine. I started learning sign language and now I didn't care why or how this had happened; I just wanted to fix it. You had such a very hard time refusing to accept it and broke all our dishes and plates behind him trying to make him hear. I felt so helpless and all I could do was hold you and dry your tears. I finally got you to use one of the signs that he and I had learned "How are you". So at last, I convinced you to try it when he responded "fine" you cried and hugged him, kissing him so hard. From then on you excelled in sign language way past me and he was learning more. We put him in the Charleston School for the Deaf. Where he excelled also. Besides the paralysis, He had no other effects from meningitis. He soon recovered from the paralysis with the teachers' help, having him walk the curb on their outings. We would forget a word and "finger spell" it to him and with your sense of humor he would sign "Look in the yellow book" (a sign language textbook). We bought a house close to a wooded area that the kids enjoyed playing in. We came out into the yard one day and the kids' pool was full of frogs, Missy had been collecting them and sitting in the middle of them. She got out with one of them and I told her she needed to let it go home to her family, so she said OK and threw it so hard on the driveway she killed it! Then she started crying. You told her it was an accident and let the others go home. Don't know why but around the same time Glen used to pee on the ants outside. Things were going okay for us. We spent our time teaching Glen and Missy sign language and raising our family. It was part of our long healing journey.

We received orders to Madrid, Spain. We sold our house and again moved into another place/country. We rented a house in Madrid about 10 miles from the Base. We had our third child Chris, the only child we planned. In our normal "fashion "of nothing going off without a hitch. You had false labor about three times and when the real one came, we were in bed, and I said let me know if it's real this time. You said it's time very loudly "He's coming! Making me fly out of bed! I had planned to see this birth; I raced through the main gate (The guard thought I was a fire truck. I had a red Fairlane). We get there and to the elevator with me in a panic and you holding your tummy. I'm pushing buttons to get us upstairs to the OBGYN and at last the door opens. In front of us above a double door there's a sign reading "Morgue"! Damn I'm on the wrong floor! At this point you're ready to deliver and I get a "Really?" I finally get you to the delivery and go downstairs to sign you in, come back and there's this spider in the doctor's hands who is my baby boy being handed to you. He came so fast there was no time for me to be there or for them to even prepare you. I see you and you're sitting in the bed and have this shit eating grin on your face saying "I told you". Of course, again the perfect mother hugging, kissing him and so proud of him. Chris was now a citizen of the United States through the American Embassy and a citizen of Spain by birth. The nurses just loved him, a baby with a Spanish name (middle name Fermin, last name Cordero) born During the Festival of "San Fermin" the day of the "Running of the Bulls" in Spain. We got him home and you of course put him on a schedule. He was so tuned into the schedule you set for him he would cry if his bath was a few minutes late, then fall asleep in it while you bathed him. The kids had a new brother and fussed over him. Remember my TDY to Incirlik Turkey for thirty days? You and the kids were waiting for me when I came home. I remember you saying, "Honey you're the only one that would come out of the ass end of a plane laughing" (It was a C130 and I came out the back ramp) No welcome home honey?? And I brought home a wood puzzle jewelry box!

It was so cool you showed me that we could tell the weather

with Chris's hair. Tight curls, Rain, Loose curls, Sunny. Remember when we were between paychecks and sort of short on money? Later you told me we had some hamburger meat that was sort of old. You made chili, fed the dog some then followed him around the house to see if he was ok. (Not knowing dogs can eat rotten meat) Then fed it to us? Ha, ha didn't know about that one for a couple of months. We hired a maid to help you and that lasted for about three weeks, and you fired her because all she did was sit around and use the phone. She came to me to keep her job, and I told her "I'm not the one you need to please". The kids enjoyed learning a bit of Spanish, important words like candy, soda and gum. It was a really good assignment. The kids made lots of friends there. We were invited to a BBQ by one of my distant cousins (on my father's Spanish side) on his ranch. It was a bit awkward at first not having ever met any of them, but they were very friendly and soon other family members came. Had great food and a great time. In our conversations, I learned more about the family history to include a copy of the family crest and that two members were Knights of the Round Table, and that the City of Cordoba was founded by the family. So now I'm telling you "I'm royalty" and you know what that means peasant. Your comment? "Don't make me lay some Choctaw on you in front of the family" so that was that.

We received orders for Davis Monthan AFB Tucson, Arizona. We settled on base with us waiting for our car to be delivered to port in Charleston, South Carolina. One morning you were making breakfast and had just finished the bacon. You poured the hot grease into a paper cup and set it aside to cool so you could throw it away like you always did and still cooking you didn't see that Missy grabbed her little stool and took it to the sink. Seeing the paper cup, she thought it was something to drink and tried. She screamed and threw the cup spilling the hot grease on her neck and chest. I heard her scream and then you scream. I ran into the kitchen from the living room and you were both sitting on the floor with you holding her and screaming "No No!". I had to literally pull you off her, rip off her pajamas and put a towel with cold water on her. We called an ambulance, and they put her in the burn unit in the Base Hospital. A friend watched the other two kids while we stayed with her as much as they let us. I caught a flight to Charleston about 11:00 in the morning to get our car coming in from Spain. I fueled and didn't stop till I was home the following day about 3: 00 PM. I picked you up and we went to the hospital. Our friends had the other two kids. After about the fifth day, We walked into Missy's room to see her and we heard her crying "Daddy help me." The medical tech was de-breeding the burn, pulling the gauze off with burnt skin. I grabbed him and threw him across the room while you went to Missy crying and holding her hands. I told him to bring me a spray bottle with distilled water now!! He did, guess I scared him. I then sat down with Missy. I used the bottle to spray the wound, softening the burnt skin. Talking to her as I wiped the blood and sprayed the area more, then I slowly peeled the gauze off with the soft burned skin. After that, each time they had to do it, that's how it was done, just made sense to me.

She was transferred out of the burn unit to a hospital room later. We came in one day and she said she wanted to see cartoons in color (all they had was a black and white TV) So I brought a small TV into the room and set it up for her. Through all of this, You felt such guilt and beat yourself up so much for not being more careful and felt you didn't protect her. You felt defeated, two of our children hurt and you felt it was your fault. I'd hold you, as you cried so hard. I told you so many times that you always put the cup against the back wall of the sink. How would you or I have ever thought Missy would reach so far for it? You carried that for a long, long time. After all the treatment was done because of her dark skin she was scared. We always made it a point to be sure she didn't feel ugly or anything embarrassing. So when kids would ask her about it, she'd say, "Oh, that's where I got burned and be okay." The three kids kept you pretty busy with learning sign language, caring for Missy in school and surprises like Chris getting out of the house and us not knowing it. My getting in the car and finding him at the main gate (about four blocks away) on his trike wearing his PJs and fuzzy slippers. I asked him where he was going, He said he was going to the store to buy a kite. So, we took him to get one. Glen got in the car somehow and put it in neutral. Taking out the neighbor's corral fence across the street. They were so good about it. We became good friends. Got a call once because Glen while out playing had gone into their house and was unloading the dishwasher (Mary was her name) was in the shower, scared her to death. They didn't have children and because of that, they decided to adopt a deaf child. I had my moments also, when Missy was still little, and I was lying on the floor tossing her up in the air with you telling me "I really wouldn't advise that as she just ate." Well sure enough, she threw up right in my mouth and face! I puked all the way to the bathroom. As I'm sitting there on the floor wrapped around the toilet bowl the heaving has stopped. Here comes Missy and puts her hands on the toilet bowl edge she pukes in the toilet now. Well hell! She got me going again with dry heaves. You again with "I told you". Another time I was getting ready for work and in comes Glen the toilet seat was up, and he put his little "manhood" on the rim to pee. Well during that process out of the corner of my right eye I saw the toilet lid coming down, I turned really fast (I was shaving) and sliced a bit of skin off my chin! Well, the toilet seat slammed down! I just stood stunned as blood poured down my cheek and neck looking at him. He was yawning and looking up at me like "huh". The pads on the lid were high enough that he was fine. Then later Chris and I on the floor played "Goat". That was a mistake with his hard head! He nearly knocked me out! Everything went nearly dark and damn my head hurt as he sat there laughing. You always told me to let the boys win whenever we would rough house. Another time I was just lying on the floor watching TV on my stomach and Glen sneaks up on me, jumps on me, grabs a handful of hair and punches me in the cheek. Oh, that was nice, I went to work and for days had to explain how my 7-year-old boy gave me the black eye. Next, I came home, and Chris was waiting in the hall, as I turned the corner he charged, and head butted me again, keep in mind he was only as tall as my groin. I Remembered that for a while. Through all these events as my children were trying to kill or injure me, your response was always "I told you so" I love your laugh and with me being so accident prone and clumsy not to mention my "accidents" I did make you laugh a lot through the years while I survived our children as well as myself.

We received orders to Hill AFB Utah. Got Glen enrolled in the Utah School for the Deaf. Our life was calm, and things were good. Kids went to the youth center, rode all over the base on the bus. I bought a dog that you wanted so badly (an Alaskan Malamute} so when the pet store called to tell us the dog is in, you were out visiting Patsy and Curt down the street (they were very good friends of ours). I went and got "Stormy" and picked him out of the litter because he had an attitude. The guy told me if you didn't like him, I could change him for another one. You came home and he was behind the drapes playing I called, and the little fat fur ball looked out and you went nuts, Oh my god he's beautiful! So that was that. You carried him all around the block to friends to see him. When he was grown, I built him a sled and he'd run through the knee-deep snow carrying the three kids and you in the back. You would take them to school each morning until the snow was gone. When he'd get out, we would go to the school to get him. He was out there playing with the kids. He was huge, but the kids knew him. He was tied to a tree on his leash in the front yard. One day when I came back, He had the tree peeled like a banana! Glad we moved out in winter, or we would have had to pay for the tree he killed. We put him out to stud once and took him to the female. After two days or so I got a call saying he won't breed. Just lays in the yard so, I go over, he sees me, jumps on her, does his business and wants to go home. Go figure... you laughed so hard telling me "Well you're going to have to hold his paw because he has to breed three times to make sure". And I did, he wouldn't breed without me there. He was such a joy but just so gentle the kids would use him for a pillow while watching TV. They would even take his bone to watch him pace until they gave it back. The little farts!

Remember the duck? I'd come back from the swap meet with a paper bag and told you this is for you. You said "Aww" and looked inside to see a baby duck at the bottom of the bag looking up at you. You said, "Gee all for me"? Well, the kids saw it, so it had a home. I built a small, fenced area for it. It grew up pretty fast I thought. Well, I had also built a worm box with bedding and all. Chris, Glen and I fished a lot. I could reach in there and in one scoop pull up some two dozen or more worms. Well, it had been a while since we fished and this day we were going to go out. I scooped up a handful out of the worm box and had maybe four worms after a few more scoops. I had maybe one dozen. When I came back from fishing, I asked you about the worm box. You said, "Well, maybe the kids fed a couple to the duck". I looked at you with a raised eyebrow and with your best sheepish "I'm sorry face" you said OK, "maybe we all did, but it was so much fun watching the duck suck them up like spaghetti". That's why that damn thing grew up so fast! About a month or so later I came home from work early, You and Patsy were out shopping, and The kids hadn't come home from school. I look out in the back yard and Stormy is just running around jumping and tossing something in the air. I walked out to the yard and it's the duck!!!!! He sees me and starts poking it with his nose. I guess trying to get it up. It used to snap at his nose through the fence, so I guess he had enough. It was deader than hell; guess he broke its neck. You come home, so I tell you about it and say you have to tell the kids. Your response? "Well, you brought it home mister!" So now somehow, it's my fault? Stormy had several litters with Chris's female Malamute; we never advertised the puppies and always had them sold. Some put down deposits before time to let them go, thanks to Stormy. People would see him and want one. Remember one time you were cleaning the fish aquarium and put your expensive glass catfish in a bowl of water and set it on the floor. One of Storms pups came in, so you picked him up to love on him and said "You smell fishy" then you looked down at the water bowl and your fish was gone. Most favorite phrase we would hear when walking him is "Oh my god" people would cross the street in front of him. You loved him and had such a way with him (as well as all animals) so even when you'd scold him, He would do things like walk over and get the TV guide, put it on the floor and rip the pages out and look at you, or go knock his water bowl over. One time you made a large roast and cut it in half to save for later. You set it on the table and walked away. Back in the kitchen you see the platter with roast on the floor, untouched with Stormy looking up at you. You said, "Well since you've already had your mouth on it, you might as well finish." He did, thank goodness you had the other half, or we would have had hot dogs or pizza for dinner. Patsy, Jenny, mom and daughter were both quite good looking (dear friends) Chris had such a crush on them both. He was maybe eleven and whenever they came over, he would make a place for himself between them and just sit there looking at one then the other. They thought he was so cute. Things were really good; You had your children at times, puppies and dear friends around you.

We Received orders to Langley AFB Virginia We lived on base housing about 10 miles from the base and settled in. Glen started school at The Virgins School for the Deaf and the other kids, the school on base. There had been a lot of break-ins so you opened the sliding door drapes so stormy could be seen since he slept in the living room. Never had a problem and you felt safe. One night you had a bunch of dried pampas in a large vase next to the wall and the wall plug failed and sparked, setting them on fire. Glen was watching TV; We were upstairs. Glen ran up after pulling the plants and drapes down and putting the fire out. (Good for Glen acting so quickly) We ran downstairs, the house was full of smoke, and at the bottom of the stairs you landed hard and broke your ankle. The base fire department determined the cause (faulty plug) and base services repaired the wall, painted and replaced the wall plug. Stormy would find a way to get out to play hide and seek with the base police, enough times that they knew him. They would offer him food and he would get just close enough then run away. I think they enjoyed the game as well. So now Stormy was a felon coming home in the back of a police car. The boys would fish a lot in a small lake there in the housing area.

Missy started hanging around with bad kids and started getting in trouble. Sneaking out, coming home drunk and at one point ran away. I guess there were times with the police (We couldn't find her. She was in another town) finally we got word they found her; they held her in custody. We went to court and the prosecutor wanted Juvenile Detention till she was 18 (she had been getting in a lot of trouble). We asked for another chance for her in a rehabilitation program for 90 days. That didn't go well as all she learned was how to live on the streets from the others, got into a relationship with another client and tried to run away. We always went to visit and would come away so disappointed that she wasn't trying. We got to take her home, skipping school and she finally got pregnant. Again, you blame yourself for how she was acting, and felt you were not a good enough mother. I explained many times she was never mistreated, well cared for and her friends were the ones who influenced her, you have done the best you could for her. You were so hurt. We talked as I'd hold you and try to ease the pain that was not because of anything you'd done or not done.

She had Wayne and married Phillip Duke. That didn't last but for a few months. She was out of the house and didn't want to come back and said that's why she said she got pregnant in the first place, but really had no choice. Things stayed rocky but we loved having Wayne in the house. He was such a joy. To this day I wonder where that loving little girl went. We used to do so much together. One day some of Glen's friends talked him into breaking into the fish shack where they sold hooks, worms and such. Well, we were kicked out of base housing. We moved to a house just outside the back gate. The boys and I enjoyed fishing off the dock since part of the base was on the coastline of the Atlantic Ocean. We would use a chicken leg and net to catch bluefin crabs and take them home, steam them and shell them, eating them with melted butter on the picnic table covered with newspaper. You always threw us out of the house because of the smell. Remeber one day Chris came home with a baby duck from a pond about three or four blocks away. He said he was alone and worried about it. So, we now had another duck. About two weeks later we heard knocking /scraping at the door. I open the door and don't see anyone then look down. There's a duck with about ten baby ducks so we put the baby duck in front of her and she turns away with all of them following her. That was an amazing thing to experience. Glen started playing football for the Virginia School for the Deaf. Their first team ever. They lost every game against hearing teams but got better each time. The marching band would come out to the field and if one stopped, they all ran into each other, some were legally blind. We would sit to watch the games and one time two kids were signing to each other, one asking the other if he got "lucky" last night. It's fun to listen to their conversations. The team did make a large article in People Magazine. Glen had two pictures in a four page article. Remember me working on my car, up on just a jack and it fell on me? Tranny smacked me in the face, and it swelled up. Geeze, I was the Squadron Safety Officer so the commander had me make a presentation to the squadron about car safety. Yes, my loving wife, you were on me like "ugly on a gorilla" worse than my commander for being so careless.

Stormy is sick now, he's old and not doing well. We talked it over with him and he says there's a lot of pain now, arthritis, He doesn't get up much anymore. We and his vet decided it's time to let him go. I don't know where to bury him as we don't want him in the trash, So I talked to my commander, and it turns out there's an officer pet cemetery on the base and since I worked directly for him. He calls the guy in charge recommending us. I met with him, and we looked at where all the pets were and found a spot under a tree at the foot of a horse. I dug the grave and made an appointment with the vet. We take him out and he's running and enjoying the play with the kids. We had second thoughts, so I called the vet. He says it's just a good day for him. There hadn't been others in quite a while. So, we take him in with all the kids, You and I hold him with the kids having a hand on him while they give him the shot. It was so fast. We took him to his place in the officer's pet cemetery with all the other officers' pets. That was so very hard on all of us. We had him since he was a pup and a real family member. We all cried over his loss, and it took quite a while before we even thought about another dog. Chris and Glen made him a marker. Later that night we lay in our bed holding each other and cried over his loss.

I got a line number for Senior Master Sergeant (E9) and came home to tell you of the promotion. You were disappointed. We sat down as I wanted to explain my plans, it was going to take one year before I put on the new rank, and I'd have to serve two more years wearing it. Also, we were prime for another overseas assignment. So, I asked you if it would be better to retire at twenty-three years. My gosh!! You jumped up, grabbed me, hugged me and were just dancing. So, I guess you wanted to retire. I declined the promotion and put in my paperwork to retire in four months. You had spent all those years as first an Army Brat (with your dad) then married me and followed me all over the country... packing up, moving and restarting in a new place, as well as TDY's (Temporary Duty Yonder) that would have me thirty to ninety days from home at a time and you never complained. Your whole life was spent in the military. So yes, it was your time to live a normal life without the military not knowing when we might move again. I thank you so much for always giving me the support and love to follow wherever we went.

We moved to California. We stayed with mom and dad for a bit then rented a house. I still had 60 days paid leave so money was coming in while I looked for work and after about a week got a job as lead foreman in an aircraft manufacturing company for small aircraft components. Missy meets Scott Zweifel and after one date moves in with him. Now she is out of the house and lives her own life. They got married. We don't get to see Wayne as much as we want to, as they live in another town. Her marriage is not good with a lot of fights and problems, we try to help but it doesn't do any good as they both have huge tempers and are young and not ready for a mature relationship. We get Chris and Glen each a car, but Glen is too busy signing to friends and not paying attention to driving so three fender benders.

It was so funny remembering the squirrels, how they would throw nuts at Chris from the trees. I came in and told you and your response as always "nuh-uh, not just once but several times. He was the only one (every time) he went to his car. We are starting to have problems with Glen as he is in a public school. There were just no deaf schools close by and we wouldn't put him in a residential school. After about two years of not getting him away from all the bad influences, we decided to move. You get word your nephew has cancer and is in the hospital in northern California. This was hard on you having to move out of state for Glen and the family.

We moved to Utah. The Utah School for the Deaf was excellent, so we bought a house and moved there. Scott and Missy followed us and rented a place in Layton. We lived in Indian Hills Subdivision. Later, they had Jess, a cute, dark-haired bundle of giggles and smiles. Chris and Glen were in school, and Chris started seeing a local schoolgirl named Brandy. He was so funny. His dates were like his first date which was to a junkyard looking for, as one example, a set of saddleback intake manifolds. A cheese and macaroni dinner in the back of a camper in our driveway and of course cruising the Vard. We now had our "Friday night" and would throw the kids out. This was our time alone to do, relax and unwind, watch TV, run around the house naked scaring the animals or an intimate night. I'd have a couple of drinks, and you would smoke one eighth of a joint (that was more than enough for you). Of course, our son Chris, always the opportunist, would knock on the door or ring the doorbell to ask for a couple of bucks, which I'd give him to get rid of him. Brandy gave him a bunny once and he came in saying it was dead, the cat killed it. I went downstairs to his room and in the crawl space and there lay the bunny. I told him it would be alright. To which he responded "Dad, the head is laying over there". Oops, Debi with that "look" at me. That look had so many sides to it. Surprise, disappointment, scolding, questioning or mad to make a point. Geeze the kids and grandkids got to know it as well. So different from your happy sweet smile.

Remember the day you came into the kitchen, (I was working at McDonald Aircraft in Salt Lake working on the Aft section of a 727) and had got off early. I was at the table eating some stew I found in the ice box, and you asked me just why am I eating the dog food? (we had a little yorkie called gunner) I go huh? You tell me Gunner didn't finish his food, so I covered it with tin foil and put it in the ice box!!! Well okay then. You walk away shaking your head mumbling "What am I going to do with you" I finished eating it, tasted like stew. You got all over Chris one day as he came down the stairs holding the dog by the front and hind legs making shooting sounds. You said, "Put Gunner down!" and Chris laughed saying his name is "Gunner". I laughed too and we quickly got the "Look".

We get word Dee, our oldest daughter (from my first marriage) is getting married, so we are going to California for the wedding. Shortly after we get word your nephew is dying from cancer, so we go to northern California to see your nephew. We come back to Utah and in a matter of weeks your nephew passes away. That was hard on you as you had spent many years together. We spent several nights in bed with me holding you, trying to comfort you. Guess we have always needed the time alone holding each other trying to work through the hard times. To help each other heal. We were each other's strength. Brandy in the meantime gets pregnant and they get married. Chris moves into her house. Later Chris calls and Brandy is in labor. We rushed her to the hospital. I put a towel down on the seat of my T bird because her water hasn't broken, and I get another "look". We get her to the ER and a few hours later we have Sam, a cute little redhead. I'm thinking red hair huh? And you quickly remind me that her mom has red hair (she is Swedish with the last name of Nestle, not that Nestle) just in case I'm going to open my mouth and say something before you put your fist in it! Mama Bear to the max. Course I loved her as soon as I saw her. Glen had moved out with some friends, so Brandy, Chris and Sammy moved in. Missy is now pregnant, and we now have little Cody, a bubbly boy. Brandy and Chris move to their own apartment in Bountiful, happy to have their "first" place. Later Scott and Missy break up and divorce so Missy, Wayne, Jessica and Cody move in. You have always loved having babies close to you and now we had a house full of them. Jessica would fuss and you'd put her in the Papa Son chair, and she would go right to sleep. She also for some reason always had stinky feet. One day you and Missy (with the kids) go shopping and Missy is just mortified because Jessy was in the cart drinking her bottle and some old man is looking at her and he says, "what a cute baby". To which Jessy says, "Get out of my face" You laughed saying "Well no one is going to kidnap her". Glen meanwhile starts seeing a girl from school named Wendy, a cute little deaf redhead and after a while the pregnant bug hits again and we have our little redhead, Darcy. They don't stay together very long. Wendy takes Darcy to California to be with her mom so it's months at a time before we see Darcy. Hard on you not to have her close. Glen is getting drunk and just won't listen to anything we try to say or do. One day Glen gets drunk, and a girl offers him a ride somewhere, he falls asleep, and she wakes him, he comes up fighting. He punches the girl badly and rips the shoulder of her shirt. The cops are right there quickly and arrest him. It's a nightmare for you and me. At his court he is sentenced to prison for fifteen years for "Sexual Assault" because of her torn shirt. We just don't know him anymore; He had no remorse. What happened was so bad and your heart was broken. Once again, you're blaming yourself. Things slowly start getting better; we have a full house of kids for you to care for and we have accepted the outcome of Glen's actions as much as it hurt. Later, Missy meets Doug and they move out into their own apartment. Brandy is now pregnant again with a boy they name Chauncey. He comes to us with a problem at birth, "transposition of the great arteries" his blood flow is backwards and he's not getting enough oxygen. That scares us all, without proper oxygen he could die! The doctors tell us there is a natural hole between the heart chambers so he is getting oxygen for now, but it will close. We call him our "Blue" baby. There was surgery to correct it, but several small procedures must be done first before the major surgery. You and I sold the house and moved to Bountiful to be closer to Brandy and Chris and get an apartment behind them because there were so many doctors' appointments for Chauncey. The procedures are to strengthen the arteries for the final surgery, to switch them to where they should be or belong. Literally cutting both arteries switching them. A very dangerous procedure that the specialists had performed before

Excerpt from Nana's Journal

Oct 7th, 1995

"Baby Chauncey was born, but something is terribly wrong. He has a heart defect, many ups and downs, many heart procedures and shunts. The Eagle would fly before each procedure but the last one.

(Added; Every time we drove to the hospital, we would see an Eagle flying.) Chauncey Cordero three and half months old. I'm in the lodge again (Added; Sweat lodge) standing in front of me is Chauncey's spirit, a beautiful diamond shaped blue in color. He would come to tell me he would be returning home! I shot out of the lodge hyperventilating: George says it's okay they (Added; Spirits) just want you to face your fears. He didn't believe it either so we both decided we would believe that. No eagle fly's March 7th it's the morning of Chauncey's heart surgery, the whole ride to the hospital I watch for the flying, but none came, that's ok I will see it late (because of course he couldn't possibly die) I'd seen this in a vision before but just pushed it away (for lack of better words) Surgery is over and time to get some rest (Added: Chauncey looks wonderful, nice and pink) The nurse says go home and get some sleep. 10:20 pm the hospital calls, we rush back but as hard as they tried the doctors could not save him. He is gone!! My heart is on the ground, this is not an option, this was never going to happen!! How could this be? Watching Chris and Brandy suffer the worst pain any parent could ever experience. So helpless, helpless anger, rage! How could you let this happen? You can fix anything! (Added: Creator). Must get to the mountains, I need to think, decide what to do. Lost, helpless, devastated, such pain. I can't do this anymore, too much pain! Who will take care of him? I must go to the spirit world. I will go there and care for him. Chris and Brandy will feel better knowing I'm caring for him.

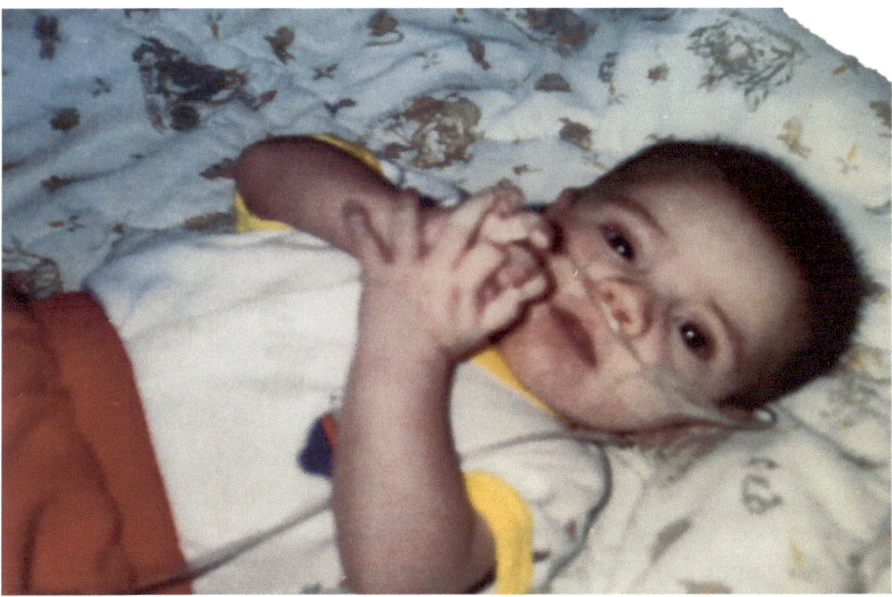

I'm alone driving in the mountains. What have I done wrong? Why has this happened? Then I hear a voice "he will return to them in another son" Oh the anger!! I'm feeling that won't help my kids now I scream!! Four Ravens came to me and gave me a gift, so much strength I never knew I could have. I began to realize I wasn't driving my car, it or something was taking me where they wanted me to go. I didn't know Darryl then, but I know I would have ended up at his doorstep had I not worried about gas. (Added: She pulled into his driveway and turned around. Later he would become our Medicine Man)

Excerpt from Nana's Journal

"Back in time, our first Sun Dance at Fort Washakie in Wyoming to support Tony and Darryl. The dance began at night, and it was cold. A little boy was shivering standing next to his mother. I put my coat on him and in that instance, I was toasty warm. I looked up at the Buffalo head on the Sun Dance tree and he came to life and moved his head back and forth looking around. What a beautiful gift I was given that night." Security was lax that night and a man took a picture of the dancers, and a whirlwind came in and hit Darryl (Added: Attacked) our Medicine Man because he was the most powerful man dancing, and he went down. It was terrible and it hurt his heart. The men got together and wanted a war (Added: They were hosting, the guest tribes blamed them) because Darryl was hit but he would not allow blood to be spilt over him. He sent his helpers (Added: Spirit) to stop it. He was a peace-loving man and a true spiritual leader. He doctored all of us to ease our pain of losing Chauncey. That is how we came to meet him."

My first Sundance was at wounded Knee under the Medicine Man Rick Two Dogs. His Alter was for Natives only, I offered my Medicine Pipe to Rick asking for permission to dance. He asked me if I had been called to dance and as I had been given the vision in sweat lodge four times, I said yes. He said he would take it into the lodge that night. The following morning, I called him and asked. He said yes it was loud and clear for both you and I to come. A month later at Sun Dance I again offered my Medicine Pipe and made my pledge of four years to pray and dance for the people and my family to heal and take my place as a Sun Dancer.

Remember how Rick intimated you? You would see him walking in camp and you'd go the other way. Come to think of it, the only Medicine Man that didn't intimate you was Darryl. At Sun Dance that year you met Lula Red Cloud, Great Granddaughter of Chief Red Cloud. You spent quite a bit of time with her talking and enjoying each other's Company. We took Jessy with us to teach her our ways. She at first was shying away from you because you were so light skinned (it hurt your feelings) until an elderly woman took her and had a talk with her about listening to her grandma and learning from her teachings.

Remember the big thunderstorm that came through? The

camp had tents blowing down and away you sat with Jessy in our tent painting her nails to keep her calm. The storm was split in two and went around the Sundance ground by Jerome and two other Heyoka. This is where she met Travis, her playmate and husband 20 years later. After a while we were blessed with another grandchild Chris and Brandy had Shelby, the cutest baby girl we nicknamed "Boo". You are told to move north and travel lightly. (again, the spirits) shortly after that we got word your mother is very sick in Alaska. So we get rid of or sell everything, (a lot to the kids) to empty out the house and get ready to go North to Alaska.

<u>Excerpt from Nana's Journal</u>

Nov 6th, 1996

"Spirits said we would move north and would travel light. Came to realize how unimportant material things are! We give a lot to the kids and sell some getting ready for our move North to Alaska. By May 1997 the whole family had come and joined us. Glen is still in prison. Important things in life: Spiritual wisdom, love and help our relations from the crawling and all in between. Humility, always be Humble. Remember the creator Wayken Tonka put as much love in creating a single blade of grass, that small plant people as he did in any of us. Respect!

We moved to Alaska. We moved into your mom's house in Big Lake to care for her. She is in the advanced stages of Alzheimer's. After a few months, we realized she needed constant care. Her doctor said she needs 24-hour care for her own safety. (Twice she walked out of the house with only a robe and slippers in 30 below weather.) She demands you stay by her side, but she doesn't recognize you anymore. Her best friend helps us sell her house because it's too much to manage. We place her in a home to have her needs met and for her safety. We find a really nice place with only five patients including herself, they have meals together, go on outings, evening gatherings and have a full-time nurse available. She loved it and we visited her often. A few months later she passed away from Alzheimer's. You were of course again heartbroken and so saddened, we released her ashes over her favorite lake in the town of Big Lake. We at that time also found out your brother Gary (also here in Alaska) had not been doing well and it was getting worse, being in a car that was hit by a train, he never completely healed. Now he was put in Hospice. Your oldest brother, Danny is also in Alaska and in the hospital for cancer treatment. A couple of months later they both pass a day after each other. In less than a year and a half you have lost your mother, and two brothers. Your heart is again so broken and you are so hurt for such a long time. So very much in such a short time is overwhelming. We release your brothers' ashes together over a valley up in the mountains. I felt so helpless and all I could do was be there and hold you. You seem so fragile now. Chris and Doug join us in an "A" frame we are renting in Sutton, our small canyon town. Both boys get jobs and shortly after send for Missy, Brandy and the kids. The "A" frame was once a children's school with 6 bedrooms and a loft, you had told them to come to Alaska and join us. Now you had your family close and the entire batch of babies. They have always been your world and a cure for any unhappiness around, it helped ease the pain of the loss you had suffered almost a year ago.

We built a sweat lodge and soon all our friends were coming to sweat once a week. Remember Bucky and his "drop byes" he would come off the slope and before he even went home, he would stop by our house, and I'd hear you say "Guess we're sweating tonight, Bucky's started the fire "so we would call everyone. Remember Malinda would bring fry bread? You called Chris who wasn't sweating that night and told him we would save him some since it was about three in the morning. Not ten minutes later he showed up afraid we would have eaten it all. Yep, it was that good. Chris and Brandy had bought a mobile home just down the hill from us, later that year Doug and Missy moved out into a place of their own also not far away. Your babies were still close enough to walk over and they were over all the time to see their "Nana". They love you so much.

Later, we moved out of the "A" frame into a trailer next to Chris and Brandy on their property at the bottom of the hill. It was hard as we had to haul water and chop wood to keep warm during the winter. It was still great for you being near the kids. I built an extension on the trailer for more room. We got a white wolf as a puppy, and all was good until he was grown and very protective of his "pack". So much so, he would attack anyone, not family. We had to put him down before he hurt someone. Remember once little Shelby came running up the drive waving a piece of paper yelling to Brandy "You can't child abuse me anymore" Brandy about died with embarrassment! Another time I remember I went with her to collect

Easter eggs at school. Well, I got hungry, so I ate one. A gold one, after the kids had gotten them all, the teacher asked who had the golden egg? Oops.... It was worth $50.00. You made me pay her for it. Christ! I bet I paid her for that egg at least 5 times!! The kids were in a lot of plays and school activities, so we went to most of them.

One Halloween we followed the hayride in our cars to warm the kids as there was about two feet of snow on the ground while they went house to house trick or treating, one little guy was so smitten with Sammy, and she just broke his poor little heart as she ignored him.

Harry Potter movies, every time a new Harry Potter movie would come out, you'd have me gather all the kids and off to the theater we would all go. When we got word a new Harry Potter book was to be released, we would buy it for the kids. The city of Palmer turned the main street into Diagon Alley with all the shops representing each shop. All the family of course had to go. It really was fun going through them. At midnight the book was put up for sale and of course we were in line.

Around the corner from our trailers, another trailer burned to the ground, so I bought the property and afterwards once the land was cleared the family and friends built a log cabin. We had the walls, all the windows and doors done. I was working on the electrical in the middle of winter. You asked why not get the heat up and running and why not move in? I'd be working to finish in warmth rather than freezing. Smart lady, so we moved in. You of course took credit for helping get the electrical in, you put the plug covers on. You so loved your cabin; you had always wanted one in the mountains. The kids would always be over. If one got sick it was to Nana's house, their safe place, they came to you for every scratch and a band aid and cough medicine.

Winters were always times to snow sled and then to Nanas for hot cocoa. Lots of birthdays, family meals, holidays, visits and seeing you every day.

Not more than two weeks after we moved in (it was not finished; I was working on it as we lived in it) twice you tried to burn the cabin down! A cigarette in the trash can in the bathroom caught the insulation on fire! The second time you came down saying "hon you really need to finish the bathroom" You're standing there with this sheepish look on your face, arms at your side with your palms up. Yes, I got the message and finished the bathroom walls for safety sake of course.

All the wildlife that was there and those that came by to be fed by you. Crows that I was so amazed that could get off the ground and squirrels that could still climb trees. They all got so fat!

Chris and Brandy had kept Chauncey's ashes and now felt it was time to let him go. Chris drove up in the mountains with us following him. He was following an owl that would stop, perch and wait for him. It led him to a flat ledge overlooking the valley below. It then hooted and flew off. We started a fire and had a prayer ceremony using our medicine pipes.

Chris opened the box and we each took a bit of ash to put in our medicine bags. Together Chris and Brandy released his ashes from the ridge to the valley below. Later Chris and Brandy gave us another Grandchild, Koby, another happy smiling baby boy. As the spirits had said (once Chauncey's ashes were released). My gosh, he was the spitting image of Chauncey! You were so very happy.

I started work as a Traditional Counselor for the tribe in Chickaloon. Remember the morning you tried to kill me? Only a couple of the wall sockets were hooked up as I hadn't finished the total electrical system yet. I was lying in bed asleep, it was morning and you were up and going to make coffee, well you needed a wall plug so you disconnected my CPAP to plug in the coffee pot. The CPAP is a closed system, so it cut off my air and now I'm flopping around like a fish suffocating, I see you with a puzzled look on your face as I'm dying!! I rip off the mask and your comment "What?"

Remember the black eye you gave me! Yep, you said "nuh uh", so I came downstairs and showed you! I went to work, and they made a poster for you as wanted for spouse abuse by the police with my picture of what you did. (it was a beauty, black and purple) I came home and put it on the ice box. You of course apologized but still didn't know how it happened. I figured it was in our sleep. We always spooned and I think you turned in your sleep and your elbow got me, don't know why I didn't wake up, unless you knocked my ass out! A few days later as I come downstairs, you're cleaning as you go by the ice box, your singing "I'm bad, I'm bad" to that song "Bad Boys", bad boys they're gonna come for you". The poster they made for you is still the icebox now.

Remember your "allowance". We had a joint checking account and of course discussed anything above the necessities like food, elect etc. to buy. So, years back you'd told me you wanted your own "mad money" so I said sure $50.00? And you stated yes $100.00 a month would be just fine. Somehow through the years that never worked out for me. We would be at the check- out and you'd pick up a few things like plants or baskets then at the checkout, I'd look at you and well? Your response "Oh honey I don't have change", "I forgot my money", "I only have a hundred-dollar bill" needless to say you seldom spent your "mad money" with me. Now if you weren't giving it to the kids, you were always spending it on them. They loved shopping with Nana.

I started working for the tribe in the law enforcement department as the Chief of Police. One day I had come home from patrol and went in the front door rather than the side door. I built some planters on the side of the porch some time back, and I see these really big nice three leaf plants growing out of them among the other flowers. After a second look, I realize they are pot plants! I ask you why you had them and where you got them. You said, you found this really nice soil just dumped out at the coal mine and brought it home and they just grew, "Aren't they pretty"? (you'd never seen the plant) my response was honey I'm the Chief of Police and those are pot plants growing on our front porch. So, you asked "Can I keep them" Geeze....

Later we got "Cubby" (the dog that wouldn't die) after being hit by four wheelers, a fuel truck and a goat that really nailed him. He had a bad case of "little man syndrome" just about anything he didn't like, he would attack around the house, finally Brandy ran over him. He was all bent out of shape, and you had a friend of yours straighten him back up. Of course, that didn't fix his bent tail Brandy had sucked up in the vacuum. In time he gets hurt by another dog and passes away. We loved that dog, and it was again so hard to lose him. It was winter and the ground was too hard to bury him, so I wrapped him in a blanket and placed him in a locked shed till summer. Later I am looking all over for my gloves to cut up firewood, I had just used them a few days after. Never find them. I'm blaming the kids. Summer comes and it's time to bury him, I take him to his little grave, open his blanket to add sage for him and I find the gloves in his blanket. Guess he wanted them, he used to play with them, so we buried them with him. Just an amazing thing to happen. Not a clue how they got there.

One evening we came home and listened to the phone messages one from Boo (Shelby) singing us the song from her upcoming play "I wov da mountains, I wov da daff o dills" still have that tape. She was so cute. The girls used to dress Koby up in girl's clothes and make up. So glad he's not brain damaged, Those grandkids!

Remember Sammy and I were fussing, teasing each other? You told me to stop tormenting that child to which she stuck her tongue out at me! I told you and Sammy states "it just fell out, it happens" … You grin and say "see". Our little Jessy was a terror in school and never took any guff so every now and then off to the school principal's office, some boy said something she didn't like, so she clocked him. Remember "don't need to worry about her getting kidnapped?" Yes, Mama bear always defends those little farts.

In time I bought you horses. Something you had always wanted. I built a corral for them. You so loved picking up "apples" for them and spending time with them. You'd get up early, go out and sit on a tree stump with your coffee and your horse Cheyenne. She would come over and nuzzle you. You loved those mornings so. One day as I was fixing the electric fence or at least trying to, Cheyenne kept biting the cuff of my pant leg and pulling me away or putting her big head on my shoulder. I had to call you to come get your horse so I could get some work done. Glen came up on parole, met and married a little Athabaskan girl named Jane and in time gave us another grandbaby named Raevyn. The kids loved playing in the dirt and sawdust pile and when little Raevyn would come over, she always left looking like a little orphan and so did her cousins. We finally told Jane not to dress her up, just put play clothes on her. There would always be a yard full of kids at Nanas.

You would take the kids on walks to the river and had been told there were bears out there but you knew the bears were your friends. Once I was with you and the kids were in a wagon, I was pulling. A huge grizzly stood up not five feet from us and you told him we were just walking through and meant him no harm. He shrugged his head, got down on all four legs and walked away. You were so calm it was amazing to see, my first thought was "I'm not armed" as my heart was racing. You have always been "in tune" with animals. You have a very special gift. Your little Sammy also has it; while standing on the porch, she would hold out her hand, call and have little chickadees land on her hand and she would actually pet them. You'd watch her from the living room window. Once little Shelby was walking to the general store, and a man stopped to talk to her, you were driving by, boy you were out of the car in a flash running him off with a few choice words. Shelby still to this day remembers your words of "wisdom" about talking to strangers.

Remember Chris and I would argue over who was taking Sammy to town when we needed to go. They were re-doing the road to Palmer and just bulldozing the trees over. Well little miss tree hugger wasn't having any part of that and would make us stop and offer tobacco for the tree people, every tree. Then one time she came in crying because her brother Wayne was mowing the lawn saying he was killing mother earth! You were there again "It's okay honey he is just giving her a haircut". Then the time the boys were cutting that tree down by Brandy's and Chris's trailer? She was telling you "Nana they didn't offer tobacco to the tree people before they started", sure enough the tree fell on the trailer and damaged the front.

The tribe soon ran out of funding for the Law Enforcement Department, so I had to shut it down. I started work as a Substance Abuse and Mental Health Counselor at a facility in Palmer. You'd always pack me large lunches with your cute/naughty notes. Friends would always come to my office asking, "What we got for lunch"? There was always enough to share.

We were doing a lot of sweats with family, extended family and friends now. You have always been intimidated by medicine people and when Buz called asking if they could come over and use the sweat because Arvol was in town? Arvol? Like ARVOL LOOKING HORSE? Of course we would be honored! You were just so very, very intimidated by him. We hosted him whenever he and his advisors came to Alaska and in time you became more comfortable around him. He would tease you a lot after your trying to shake his hand wearing a kitchen mitt (you were cooking) food for after the sweat. You did really look forward to being in a sweat with him, powerful.

Cody meets Rebecca and in time gives us another grandchild, Oliver, a beautiful boy. Remember the "birds and bees" talk you gave those two when they were dating? You couldn't sleep so you tried "Ambien", and it was about 9:00 at night. I heard you and came downstairs. You were sitting on the stairs and Cody and Rebecca were at the foot of the stairs. You were talking to them for some 30 minutes. I finally told you it was time for bed and took you upstairs. You didn't remember anything the next morning...

Later things just don't work out for Brandy and Chris and

they divorce. Chris goes to work on the railroad in Arkansas. Brandy in time meets Rex and they marry, she sells the property and together they buy a house. They moved to Palmer, so we don't see the kids as often. I went to see my mother in California, it had been several years since I'd seen her. You had decided to stay and suggested I take Jessy, so we went for a week. While there her father, Scott called and asked to see her. Scott and I had had our disagreements in the past but by no means about Jessy or Cody, so they got together for the first time and really bonded. He took her to meet the rest of his family, and it was really great to see them so together, as a matter of fact, we didn't see much of her after that. This had not happened before because of Missy, neither Jessy nor Cody had an opportunity to meet him. We came back to Alaska, and they continued to stay in contact. Later when she married Travis in Alaska he flew up and walked her down the aisle and gave her hand in marriage. Scott, Debi and I communicated a lot as well about his kids. He passed in 2024 which devastated Jessy and Coby. They only had 17 years together, as father and children. I'm so sorry they didn't have more time. The picture is of his sweet little Sadi, his granddaughter after his funeral. Jessy of course had gathered the family to mourn and heal.

I changed jobs and started work as the Director of the Hudson Lake Substance Camp. Its only access is by float plane or four-wheeler in the summer months and snow machine in the winter. Part of the program is substance living so we hunted and fished very little outside food. We went to Sundance at the Horse Camp in South Dakota. It's Chris's first dance under Ben Rhood. You remember you were walking back to camp, and you and Melinda, Bucky Mean's wife, passed each other, stopped, turned and ran into each other's arms. So good to see you and her together again. I changed jobs again because it was two weeks in camp and one week out. Plus putting out fires from the camp even when I was home. Not enough time together. I started work as the manager of the Prison Substance Abuse Program and after 2 years or so we decided to sell our cabin and move. Winters had just gotten too hard for us.

We Move to Arizona. The weather is hot, really hot, one hundred and ten degrees! Getting off the plane we thought we had died and gone to hell! Chris had married with his wife Shana and they were living in Casa Grande Arizona, so we joined them for a short time then bought a house in Arizona City. I think this is where you had a stroke. You didn't wake me and just pushed through it. As time went on, I started to see weakness in your left hand.

Our little Ginger Sammy came down and was living with her dad and Shana in Casa Grande. Now you have one of your grand-children back and spend a lot of time with her. Jessie meanwhile gets married to Brian and comes to visit from Alaska with our new little great granddaughter, Sadie and spent two weeks with us visiting the sights of the Grand Canyon, Meteor Crater, etc.

You complained the kitchen sink won't drain. I use drano, plunger, and a snake and nothing. So, I crawl under the sink and take the trap off and a section of drainpipe, I get up and show you solid lard in it and I say you plugged it all up, your response "nuh uh". Now you admit you have been emptying hot grease down the drain with hot water so it should have been okay. I explain honey, hot water is not as hot as grease, and it turns SOLID in the pipes when water hits it.. "Ohhh you say sorry, but I knew you would fix it though."

You always loved your yard sales, Goodwill and Bishop's Attic looking for "treasures" I remember you brought home this four-legged footstool, it was badly stained with a hole and some of the foam padding missing, stain faded and loose as hell. You gave me your "treasure" and ask me honey "fix" it (one of your many projects). Soooo I stripped it down, glued and added screws, reupholstered and re-stained it. You loved it saying, see a treasure! Such a deal! I explain to you that I just spent the better part of a week and about $30.00 in supplies to fix it! Your response, "but honey it only cost me $3.00" I always loved your logic. So, you got a wonderful deal for only $3.00... Sammy meets a guy and starts dating him. Things seem serious. She's working at Fry's Market, and all has been going well for a while. But then problems come, she gets pregnant, and the guy turns into a control freak and is trying to run her life, as well as the baby. He is out of control. At this point Sammy gives him no say as she feels that without him in her or the baby's life, they are better off. We all agree with her and help her move back to Alaska to have our little great granddaughter, Emmy. He still tried calling the hospital telling them how he wanted things done. The hospital responded that since they are not married, and his name is not going to be on the birth certificate the conversation is over. She has Emmy and a very good friend, Rayn is with her. Fifteen years later, they are still together and have asked her father, Chris to marry them.

A few months later Chris goes to Texas to work with Shana's brother, Brad and is making good money, so they decide to move to Cisco Texas. It doesn't take long before you need the kids, so we put the house up for sale. We have only been there about two years. The house gets sold to friends of ours, Cody Blackbird (The Cody Blackbird Band) had stayed with us twice during his tours and had really liked the house so when we put it up for sale, he wanted it. He and his brother bought the house for themselves and their father. So, we are moving to Texas.

We move to Texas. Chris finds an empty lot across the street, and we buy it, shortly after Chris comes to help us pack up and then we head to Texas. We came in a moving van and a small motor home. We parked on the side of Chris's house and hook up to water, electricity and the internet. So now with the moving van parked on our property and us across the street with Chris. Boo (Shelby) and Koby come to Texas to stay with him, you're happy again. We spent about four months in the cramped camper with kids all the time.

Chris, Shana, I, Brad and his son help build a shed on our property and move all our belongings into it. I then turn in the moving van and shortly after that the mobile home we bought is delivered. We had cleared the property and leveled it out so they could just bring it in. Oh my gosh but we were so happy to move our belongings in and get out of the camper! You have all your things around you, your great grandchildren all over the place again. The kids have started school and Boo accelerates and graduates. She is so much like you and so easy to embarrass too. Remember the time in Walmart and we were in the clothing section? I hold up a pair of Speedos and ask her in a loud voice Shelby, "Do you think these would make my ass look too big"? She turned beet red. Then another time we went out to eat at the Mongolian Buffet and I took a baby octopus and put just the head in my mouth with the legs hanging out, she just turned so green. I really felt sorry after because I thought she was going to chuck. Not to mention your "look" and kick under the table. Koby fights school at first and one day the coach tells him he's going to play football. Didn't ask, just told him. He just takes off, grows, and becomes an "A" student and a star football player. He's known as "Alaska" and the coaches from teams they play against had a lot of respect for him, almost always "double teaming" him to try and keep him off the quarterback. Koby is offered a scholarship for football, but he wants to do something other than football. He graduates and goes to work in the prison. He wants Law Enforcement. Then later joins the Air Force as Security Police working towards specialized security.

We buy you a little mini and put him in a fenced area by Chris's house. You just loved the little guy. You're now diagnosed with advanced Parkinson's Disease. It was hidden by the stroke and you're not as steady on your feet. In time you're telling me he needs a friend to play with, so we got you another one and now the fenced area is too small, so we complete the fence on our other property next door to the house. They run all over having a ball. You play with them and just sit enjoying them. You are getting sicker and in time we must let them go, because I can't care for them and it's getting much harder for you as well. You tire easily and are not really steady on your feet. You're getting Physical Therapy, and it helps some.

Brandy had come down from Alaska and moved in next door on our property in a little house soon after we got a mobile home and attached it to the house.

Boo in time meets and is dating Dave and later we are blessed with two great grandbabies little Jack and Sheyenne. Later they break up over his control issues and complete lack of any sense of fatherhood. Later Boo starts seeing Doug and we have more little great grandbabies, little Nikki and Kaison. They buy a house together and over time, It also has problems with a lack of husband/fatherhood responsibilities. Brandy's place next door becomes a fenced play yard with swing set, pool and run wild area for all the great grandkids. Jessy divorced Brian and sometime later met Travis in Alaska (the two met as children twenty years ago in South Dakota) They soon married, and we have another great grandchild, our little Milli. Now all but three of the grandkids and great grandkids are here with you. They moved here to Texas and stayed for about two years then moved back to Alaska. In the meantime, we get to have another bonus granddaughter, Hailey, Travis's daughter. She becomes part of the family. Something you have always loved is the way the kids always followed us all through my military career and retirement. Our "movie nights" and of course popcorn and fly's that you always provided.

Meantime since coming to Texas, I seem to be more accident prone. First after some thirty three years of not only handling but carrying firearms. I'm cleaning my gun and I shot my finger off in a "farm accident". I'm looking at my hand thinking "that's not going to grow back" You call Chris telling him "Dads shot himself" (yep I shot my finger off) he gets me to the ER. No, didn't grow back. As with the kids, you comfort me with "it's going to be ok" then I see your look knowing my firearms possession may be in danger.

Next, I'm going to fix Brandy's roof, fall off, and as I lay there thinking when I get my breath back, That's someone else's job. Later that night, I'm in so much pain and in a cold sweat. You call Chris and he will take me to the ER. They check me over and can hear blood in my chest. Very quickly they put me into surgery, and they found my spleen ruptured and about 6 quarts of blood in there. Chris told me I was circling the drain. So far I've lost a finger and spleen, not doing so well. Brandy gets married to Jose and that doesn't work out at all, he ends up in jail for domestic violence.

You're getting sicker now and I can see you having so many physical problems. I care for you more and more as you're becoming unable to do very much for yourself and you're always apologizing for needing so much. You are always worried about others, I keep telling you that anything I do for you, you would gladly do for me. I'm always looking for ways to make things easier for you, buying equipment, appliances, anything that helps. They help make you more comfortable, but your health continues to decline. The stroke and Parkinson's are ravaging your nervous system and body. I'm helpless to stop fighting it in any way I can. You're less mobile and are spending more time either in the recliner or bed and in a very short time become bedridden. There are no more medicines or doctors that can do anything to help us. I care for you twenty-four seven. Sleeping less, stressed more and trying to keep you comfortable. You of course are apologizing and hating my having to do so much for you. I keep telling you I love you and anything I do for you: you would gladly do for me and more. Chris tells me of someone who has some 10 years' experience in health care working with Shana, his ex-wife. I asked her over and you and I are impressed with her. I ask Char (Char Lopez) if she could help a couple of times a week when she's not working. She agrees but refuses payment. After a couple of times here with us Chris asks how it's going, and I tell him she's perfect. Debi likes her and she's very attentive, knows what she's doing and spends a lot of time reading to you, watching TV, joking, helping you exercise and helping me with the house. Chris tells me she's getting a divorce and has been looking for a place of her own to get away. I tell Chris to ask her to come over, I tell you about it and when she comes over, you ask her if she would consider moving in here to our spare bedroom. There were few places to rent so she asked how much. I told her in exchange for room and board, she could move in full time and when not at work,she would continue to help us. She was stunned that we would ask her and said yes. She only worked about three times a week but was home by 7:00 PM or so. She helped care for you and helped me, it didn't matter the time.

Doctors now are recommending Hospice for nursing care and meds. This is so very hard for me, I felt like I would be giving up and giving your care to someone else. As it turned out, with Char and I here taking care of you the nurse wasn't needed to administer your meds. I had already bought all the equipment including the bed so all she needed to do was monitor your meds. You have started sleeping more and have become more inactive. We're getting you up as much as we can, but you're sleeping more and want to be in bed. As those short months pass you sleep more and are always in pain. The nurse and I talk, and I must agree to raise your pain medication.

She also tells me your organs are starting to shut down, that's a punch in the gut! so the medication now is to sedate you. I'm going crazy and spend a lot of time in the shower helplessly crying, I'm losing you and can't stop it. Your nurse says now it's a matter of days and then hours as you're heavily medicated in an induced coma. I lay in bed with you telling you how much I love you and I'm telling you it's ok to rest as my insides are screaming. This is a living hell knowing the time is coming and there is nothing I can do to stop it. Pleading and praying brings no comfort. So utterly helpless.

Char took time off as well as Chris. They are here every day and were with me when your passing came. Char grew to love you, and you loved her. She cried with Chris and I when you passed.

This is where I lost you on the 9th of June 2022 at 1:52 PM. Your children and grandchildren from Alaska and California joined us via zoom for your memorial and pipe ceremony. I have been trying to piece my life together to bring some sort of personal joy back. But it's so very hard to do when you were the source of all my joy, happiness, tenderness, laughter and love which all flowed out into my world. We have children and grandchildren who loved you so deeply and knew you for all those things. Our great grandchildren will not have the chance to grow within your love and that also is a loss I will see. I miss you; I think about what more I could have done to give you the life you deserved and do feel I could have done more. The little things like telling you more often how beautiful you are, not just dressed up but in blue jeans, hair pulled back picking up horse apples in the corral. Hugging and kissing you much more often. Just holding hands, walking, being silly and laughing with you. I no longer wish when I sleep in our bed, that I would not wake up. I know you want me here to help care for our children, that has always been the passion of your life. The deep love of your children and family. I will be with you again when my time is up. No man could have had a better life than the one you've given me. When I'm called, I lacked nothing.

Our Memories

Husband, George

I want to put this down from me to you, to tell you how I'm feeling. It's been about a year and a half since you passed. While I know you're no longer in pain for which I'm so grateful. I am still feeling so much anger and disbelief that you were taken from me so young. I would offer my life for yours without hesitation if I could, your children need you. I get lonely Debi, I know there are people and family that care and love us. I just can't get used to the world going on like nothing has happened. I just want to scream to the world about the loss of your beautiful soul! My life! Your physical presence is gone, so much of my life and purpose is also gone, caring for you and loving you was my only job every day.

I'm asked to go fishing or shooting with Chris and Koby and I have to force myself to go out, even to a simple dinner. Then there's that uneasy feeling in my stomach thinking I need to be home because you may need me. It's a habit I know but maybe that explains where I am. Standing still and wondering what I'm supposed to do next. I miss your smile: your laughter and you're singing our silly song with me. I lay in bed, our bed and l look around seeing what you saw every day, your house which you loved and how you have it decorated, your things all around. I ache for the feel of your hugs, reaching over during the night knowing you're lying close to me, going to sleep spooning. Getting up and asking you if I'd told you I love you today and your response of "yes, but you can tell me again"

The cute way your face would go when you cringed over something that you didn't like. Calling each other "silly La La" over things we didn't want to do. Sometimes it gets so very hard having this emptiness that I feel, the ache always just under the surface, waiting to come up and when it does, it comes hard, a place, a picture or a song like "All Alone Am I" by Brenda Lee that one just emotionally hits me so hard, as it says all I feel. I still open your urn to add a rose petal and prayer from the bouquet on your Birthday, Anniversary, Valentine's Day or just because I want them there. Sometimes I just sit quietly with my hand over your tattoo as the ink holds your ashes in it. I know you're not there but it's all the physical presence I have left of you. Those nights on the sofa or bed watching Hallmark movies, they always seemed to bring tears to you. Yes, me too. I think about how you made me laugh every day, sometimes at myself, you or our kids. Every day was fun with you, we were always laughing about something.

I do get out of the house with the kids more to have dinner or a movie somewhere and it is fun being with the kids. That gut feeling is still there, and I do look forward to coming home. Our house is my refuge I guess, with all the craziness out in the world in our house, you are still around me and the rest stays outside. These are all things that will come to pass, I know it will become easier, but never forgotten. I don't feel sorry for myself because in my own world, in our relationship, what we shared, so much laughter, joy, love and of course heartbreak and loss. I will always feel I got so much more than I ever gave. You filled my days completely. I do look back often and think of those days and years we shared, smile with so much gratitude to have had you in my life, some day without the pain.

Always, your loving husband
George

Granddaughter, Shelby (Boo) Cordero

I wanted to write this down because I don't think people understand. I'm probably one of the luckiest people in the world because I got to see something hardly anyone sees these days, and not only did I get to see it, but I have lived in it for 27 years and going. True love. I got the luxury of seeing what true love is in its most beautiful form. Two best friends sharing their lives together. I got to experience the most beautiful, compassionate, goofy, heartwarming emotional relationship on this planet. Nobody wants anything serious anymore because nobody wants to put in the time and effort. Everyone has become selfish and greedy. I was lucky to see what might be, two people who were truly selfless. Who took the phrase "you and me against the world" and lived it every day. I got to experience how people should treat the ones they love, how through the worst and best of times they did it together and never turned their back on each other. A love so rare and beautiful I could only hope to experience a fraction of it for myself. A love that truly never dies because even after her body gave up, he still loves and cherishes her soul every single day. He still takes care of her and thinks of her and lives through her. They say till death do us part. That isn't the case here, even in death their love is so inspiring, this is the most beautiful thing to witness, and I am the one who has that luxury. You can't understand true love like this unless see it firsthand and I'm so grateful to my Grandparents for allowing me the honor to be part of their lives.

Love you both,
Shelby

<u>Granddaughter, Jessy Marie Brown</u>

My Dearest Nana,

      The kindest soul, and warmest heart. A smile made our day start. "it's going to be a happy day" you'd say. Dancing through your chores, in a perfect home- You liked it kept that way.

      I feel you in my own home, when I tidy it just so. A kind reminder that you're still here-even though we had to let you go.

      I think about you every day. The little things like Diet Coke, and big beams of sunny rays. Your teachings echo in my head, reminding me to walk our ways-I still hear your laugh and feel your warmth, it keeps my fears at bay.

      Your light touched every inch of the room-though you were too humble to know. I'm grateful for you always, for teaching me that glow.

      My heart is light because of you, my first thought is to be kind. You always took the highest road, even when it's hard to find.

      This world seems dull without you here, but I know you don't go far. Because making us all feel your love, is still just who you are.

      Nana, you were the light of my world. Pilamaya, Tehilalla, forever your "little black-haired girl".

Love you,
Jessi Marie

Seraphina and I
(Great Granddaughter and Granddaughter)

Granddaughter, Raevyn Crane

Fond Memories: Summertime in Sutton Alaska was always a fun joyous time for me. Hearing that I was going to Nana and Tatas always made me squeal with joy and I'd be excited for hours until I got there. I was always greeted by a warm happy smile from Sidekick and a few good yaps from Cubby their dogs. I was obsessed with patch's the cat because of this, to this day I still love cats. After my animal greetings, Nana always gave me a big hug. I thought my cousin Shelby had the coolest knick-knack cat collection; the horse corral was magical. I still remember Nana putting me up on Choctaws back and feeling like I was on top of the world. She was such a sweet horse too.

You would always find food from the last meal left out for the ancestor's spirits, l still love that practice. You could always count on tight warm hugs, the brightest smiles, yummy snacks and food, kisses for your boo boos and refreshment for your soul. Nanas and Tatas was always the best place to be. The sweats might as well have made it an all-inclusive spa for soul and body.

I would play pretend Harry Potter, stick wands and spells memorized with my cousins Coby, Jessy, Sammy, Wayne and Shelby, have tea parties and play with dolls and stuffed animals. Nana would set up a Harry Potter movie, make popcorn and flies, hot cocoa and M&Ms or other favorite candy as we all laid on our blankets and sleeping bags on the floor in front of the TV, such fun nights.

I remember the many times Nana would have us ride ponies and horses to the Sutton General Store, the cheese fries were phenomenal. Coloring while waiting for our food at dinner was top tier and the music set the mood.

Trips to the amusement park always included a gallon of milk and Hershey's chocolate bars to make homemade chocolate milk while we played, fun car rides listening to "Savage Garden" the short car rides were the best ones, car full of us and you were told to stay down so no one sees you? And you're in the very back where there's no seat, you became a giggling bag of groceries, and it was always bumpy and fun. Nana had the best collection of Native American dolls, I really love her taste in furniture, particularly the bear coffee table. I always thought it was so cute. It was not just summers that were fun, when we were not riding the wagon down the hills we were racing sleds in the snow, making snowmen, shoveling snow, making snowmen, shoveling snow, making snow forts and having snowball fights, Nana was always right there with us, always. It was always a special treat when Nana would make us honey bear lollipops. Our nights in the sweat lodge with Tata and us all, they were so magical, and I miss them. I miss your hugs and sweet reassuring voice; these memories will forever be with me as the most fun times of my childhood. I am so fortunate to have had a Nana who saw the importance of showing us our families' traditions and culture. Those I will never forget, having us cousins, aunts and uncles hanging out together, the bonds and love were important to everyone.

Seeing this as I wrote it down, I note the things I need to make sure I'm on top of these as the years go on, so that our children have those meaningful relationships with the people we love. Lessons my loving Nana taught us all.

Much Love,
Reavyn Crane

Grandson, Cody Zweifel

One of my favorite memories of Nana is all of us getting together as kids watching movies and eating popcorn and fly's at the cabin. It is probably the best part of my childhood was when we were all so close and family. I would hang out with my relatives and family members on a regular basis. No matter how bummed out one of us was, Nana would dedicate a day to each one of us to make us feel better. We would go thrifting looking for treasures, no matter how gloomy a day was, Nana always found joy and the light in life. I miss this and much more. She was always bringing us together and always being there for me when I needed her the most, as well as the rest of us kids.

I love you Nana,
Cody

Grandpa, I've been thinking of the memories I have of Nana which have been both difficult and easy. I miss her and when I think of her of course some of those core memories come to mind. Sledding for hours, Harry Potter or Scooby Doo. Really movie nights in general with popcorn and flies. But there are also the little things that come to mind often. Small triggers that remind me of her. How she was my comfort, how we used to garage sale together and the thrift stores. Her pure joy at sales and finding "treasures". Nana dates were the best, they always included skipped school days, lunch and a toy. Usually followed by a "don't tell anyone", making it feel that much more special. There was also the advice she always gave me on Life, Spiritual and relationships. Ha, Ha it was endless but always with such caring. She loved to talk on our walks or drives. I think I got that from her, I find I do the same thing when it's just Emilly and I on car rides.

She was always there for us; it still feels that way in situations I know I'd normally feel scared or stressed, I feel a sense of calm. I imagine her with me, and it seems to help. Our lives weren't perfect, but they felt that way with her. When we were sick, she was all we wanted because she took such great care of us. When we were in trouble too. I personally remember crying and repeating "I want to go to Nanas"!! Probably because at Nana's I was never in trouble. She helped me with heartbreaks both learning love and relationships, family or friend issues.

My memories of her protection are strong. She was so strong and independent yet somehow so feminine. The balance she had of Lion and Doe in balance. She would appear soft, until someone messed with us or spoke ill about us and the Lion was let out and she didn't care who saw it.

The patience and joy she had making sure all of us kids were having a great time even if it meant she had to stand at the bottom of the snow hill in the cold while we sledded then hot cocoa after, or sit at a park table while we played, always watching us, or I don't know, refilling our bathtub a million times with hot water from the stove so we could stay warm and splash it all over the bathroom floor of the trailer even though she would remind us repeatedly to keep the water in the tub. Do you remember my own "Bernie Box"? I loved crafts and all our "Bernie" boxes had anything you could imagine to make stuff. She made mine at least 5 times over. I left mine out in the rain once, and she was pretty upset and I felt bad, but she made me another one. Which brings me to another lesson of hers, forgiveness. She once told me she wasn't very good at it, but I believe she was better than she thought. Another memory I have its small and silly but when I'm in the car driving and a good song comes on, like a certain cowboy (Josh Turner) that you may or may not have deemed us senior and junior hussies as we sang alone with it; I'll tap the steering wheel while I sing it, and it always reminds me of her.

She always had her nails painted pink; it was kind of a staple of hers. She didn't wear a lot of makeup; she was classy and went for a more natural look. Usually, mascara and lipstick. She always had her nails light pink, I'd never seen her paint them but somehow they were always done and never chipped!! She would get down and dirty too. With the animals, like the horses, pets, cleaning, dishes and no nail polish chips. How did she keep her nails like new?? Just one of Nana's many secrets I suppose. I shower once or do a single dish and nail polish chips!

I remember Nana always sort of humming, I love to sing. I can still see her smiling and humming in the cabin kitchen. Richard Simmons, that work out guy. Yep, we had a few work out sessions. Then she would break out her house cleaning songs like "The Night Chicago Died". She liked the little things, I really loved that about her. Oh, how I remember when I'd sleep over I'd wake up and have a cup of coffee and cigarette on the coffee table waiting for me. She was always so thoughtful with us. It was always so funny when she would bring in 30 or so bags of groceries and Cubby would know which bag had his new toy in it, along with a new Ninja movie for Koby.

You two weren't super affectionate in front of us but your love still shined brighter than most. The kisses in the kitchen, or when you'd get home from work holding each other's hand. Or a sweet surprise from you of some kind, flowers, food or gift. My all-time favorite is you two singing "is you is, or is you not, my baby". I love how she'd also play being so tough on you. Seeing you guys laugh I guess isn't a personal memory, but it is one I so enjoyed. Gramps, I have so many memories of Nana. How do I write a lifetime down? She is a big part of who I am today. I haven't even touched on the Spiritual side of her that we shared and her teachings. When I think of who I am, of being native and what that means and how to walk that path. I'm always thinking of her. I think of holding her hand in the Sweat Lodge, her gleaming telling everyone when I went further in the rounds. I think of the Medicine Pipe ceremonies with her and her prayers. I think of our nature walks and the way she would relate to mother earth and us, our bodies and hers. Listening to our Uncle Paul and Medicine Dream playing in the cabin or my attempts at mediation which to this day I still have not figured out well lol. Being head-to-head with a buffalo on my last meditation journey with her and how she simply laughed and said spirits have such a sense of humor.

I remember sitting at a table in a restaurant and I suggested that maybe all the other planets are bare and unlivable because we did that? Maybe the creator keeps giving us more chances and we keep ruining the planets? She was super impressed when I thought of that. Another lesson she taught me to see further. Oh my gosh! My book I wrote for reading rainbow about littering. I don't remember about the contest itself, but I remember Nana helping me write it and being proud of me. She was always so good at supporting and loving us. She made it feel like the weight of the world wasn't so heavy and anything was possible. You always made us believe in ourselves always.

I Love you,
Sammy

Grandson, Koby Cordero

If I had to describe Nana in one word, it would be "peace" . She was the glue that kept us together and the core of us all. I have so many memories with Nana, but the most memorable moments were when she was there at our lowest. She always fought for us, no matter who or what it was up against. There would've been nothing that she would have let harm our family. I will forever be grateful for my Nana. She was definitely one of the biggest factors that helped mold me into the man I am today.

I'll never let go of the memories she created with us. Whether it was walking down to the river, or sledding down a snow-covered hill, finding garage sales, pawn shops, or trips to Bishop's Attic looking for "treasures". Those will forever be ingrained in my head. I will forever be grateful for the time I got to spend with her and the never-ending love she showed me throughout my life. She truly was a kind and loving soul.

Love you,
Koby

Son, Chris Cordero

Mom,

The woman who raised me, protected me and disciplined me when needed. My mother had the courage of a wolf, the wisdom of the Raven and the strength of the Bear. My mother was Mother to many even those who were not blood. She gave without expectations and forgave those who didn't deserve it. She always showed me the kind of person I thrive to be and reminded me daily of the better person I can be. I fail and fail but I always hear her voice pushing me forward showing me the correct patch. Even now in her absence I see her everywhere and hear her lessons in everything I do.

My mother was a teacher to many, a provider and protector. She did everything with 100% care and giving.

Always a loving person and although her time with us was cut short, her teachings and her love lives on in us, her children, grandchildren and great grandchildren as well as the many who knew her. She believed in every one of us. Even when one of us would get on the wrong path, she would never give up on them. She strived to help them and guide them and to show them the right way. She would be firm but gentle and did her best even being heartbroken at their choices, but she would never give up on them. My mother loved life and time with her family. She loved watching while Dad and I worked together. When she was around, she was always laughing and joking. We never had a bad day at work with her around and she'd say we were her best entertainment. She had such a great sense of humor, and it would radiate through all of us.

My mother had the greatest love of animals and nature, she gave as much care and love as she would to family pets. All the wildlife that simply lived near her home would be well fed from spirit plates and treats, we had squirrels that could barely climb and birds that could barely lift off for flight, moose that came back each year to have their baby bedded down under the kitchen window. You can bet they all made it through the long hard Alaska winters.

She was everyone's Mother; she was my Mother. The best anyone could ever have.

I love you Mom,
Chris

Chris
Son

Son, Glen Cordero

My memory. I have not forgot how my mom took care of me. I keep think of when she used wrong sign language and I tell her see book make me laugh, she always learn sign language same thing with my dad and brother. She always there for us, do things make us happy when sad. I ask mom to take to dance or skate and she always make time for us. The time in sweat lodge with family and others learn. Mom always teach me about spirits and the mother earth and about respect of the living things. When baby born, Mom always there to see and help always, she say about family. Mom always support like brother and sister sign language. I remember what she say about to be good person. Help others and family. I really can't think of what else to say so much good memory. It hurt to say, miss and love her so much. I wish mom good heaven spirits.

I love you Mom,
Glen

Daughter In Law, Brandy Cordero

My Memories of an amazing woman, Debi Cordero or as I would come to call her "Mom" I came into the family by flirting back and forth over the fence with Chris, mom's son. We started going out on dates to the junk yard instead of going to school. We had a date in a little camper in the driveway and had mac and cheese and hot dogs. Before long Chris and I marry, and I'm in labor with our first child, Samantha who now I feel is coming! So, we rush to Moms and Dads. Dad is then announcing, "not in my T bird". Moms doing the GEORGE!!! Thing and we all know mom and her famous GEORGE!!! So, she says we are going in your precious car... If we would have had diapers, we would have used them, so instead mom put a lot of towels down just in case my water broke. So I'm in labor, in the delivery room, hungry and hurting and moms doing the mom thing trying to do what she can to comfort me. Then here comes dad with a bucket of K-fry, sits down and starts munching away in front of me!!! Mom, GEORGE!! You can't bring that in here... Well, you know dad "watch me". One of my best memories because it was so cool. On the base they have a store called the BX and during Christmas time we all went there to go shopping. Mom and I went wandering, looking for Oriental décor and we found this beautiful cork that was carved into something really pretty and I said how much I loved it. We left and I asked Chris if we could go back so I could get it for mom for Christmas, he said that she would love that, but we had to wait for Chris to get paid. Well payday all excited, we went back to the BX and it was gone. We were bummed. Well because Mrs. Samantha Cordero was Chris's first-born mom who went nuts on Sammy's first Christmas. I think there were actually a couple of toys that she bought twice because she forgot she had bought them, So much stuff. So Christmas 93 we all did the presents and she had a couple for me and when I opened one it was that Oriental thing we wanted to get that was gone. Mom had bought it for me, I was so happy and it was amazing, yelling ohh that's what I wanted to get you mom! I told her to keep it, you said no I got it for you.

Chris and I kept busy with extra activities and moved out of mom and dad's place to one of our own. I became pregnant again with Chauncey right after having Samantha. 94 was probably one of the worst years for us all. We were all a mess; things were pretty stressed and sad behind the scenes with what we were going through. Mom and dad were learning more of their heritage and practicing their Native American Ways.

Chauncy was in the Primary Children's Hospital. We found he had TGA (Transposition of the Great Arteries) . This heart condition was taking its toll on the whole family because we didn't know what from one day to the other was going to happen. Mom and dad were doing sweats praying to help Chauncey.

Christmas time, Chauncey was able to come home for a couple of days, mom was of course smothering him with kisses. His oxygen levels dropped so Chris called 911 and he was transported back to Primary. Mom made prayers and smudged him as well as all of us. We were all so stressed and worried. Not knowing again what would be happening. Chauncey had the surgery and looked good. He relapsed and passed March 95. We all were hurt so badly. Mom of course was in shock as well and left in the car for a while. Later we met Darrell who was to become our Medicine Man. Mom wanted us to go to see him and the whole family went to him for healing.

Mom and dad were doing ceremonies and participating in their native ways a lot now. We were making trips from Utah to Idaho to buy lotto and scratch offs and they got them (mom, dad and Chris) into this weird, or as I would come to dread "roadkill" thing it was ugg!. Every time on the road they would spot a dead hawk or anything that didn't bark or meow. It was fair game and would come home with us.

Mom heard her mom was sick and had been told before to go north. Her mom was in Alaska, so Dad and mom made the decision to go... Later in 97 the whole family, me Chris, Sammy, Shelby, Doug, Missy, Jessy and Wayne joined mom and dad. The best decision ever and of course it was like heaven for roadkill. So much wildlife. Mom was always walking down to the river with the kids while I was working. She would come in after for her sugar-free sobe green tea, and of course the kids anything they wanted, it was a general store so of course snacks, drinks, cheesy fry's, the sky's the limit as long as dad didn't know she was putting it on their tab. I was always worried they were going to get eaten by a bear but her reply was "don't worry I dropped tobacco for them." Mom absolutely loved having people over for sweats, she really thrived on having people around her on the same spiritual path. She would go above and beyond for the potluck after to make the sweats a great experience for all who attended. During this time, I had gotten into a relationship with "Satan" and felt everyone was growing kind of apart. I thought it was love but mom saw right through his BS. She called me a couple of times, crying, begging me to find someone else. It didn't tear our relationship apart but did take its toll where it was easier to drift apart. It went on for 10 years after which I wound up losing our home. I fell hard into a hell of a head space. Years go by and another failed relationship.

I called mom and dad asked if I could come for a visit. I ended up staying. They helped me regroup and now I have my own little spot with family all around again. Mom was an amazing mother to me. I will never forget all the happy funny moments we shared. There are so many. She was a protective Nana and would and did tear anyone apart to protect. She always would do whatever she could for anyone of her kids, grandbabies and great grandbabies. You are so loved and missed mom.

Love you Mom,
Brandy

Grandkids Memory Chain

Sam: How would you guys feel, (gramps) about doing a memory chain? Doesn't have to be significant but detailed memories we have of our time with Nana? We all loved her, but our experiences, perspectives and memories are all unique and different.

Jess: Remember our Harry Potter movie dates our whole herd always went to see the new one then to fireside when the book came out.

Jess: I have so much here... All my Harry Potter stuff... The Christmas ornaments she collected from Bishops. She will always be with me.

Jess: Sam's fault she drove into the dirt mound in the construction zone.

Sam: Ha-ha oh my gosh! She sees it, she sees it, she doesn't see it!

Tata: Seem to remember when you became teens you two would always get in trouble Sam

Sam: Whaaaa?? Me? Nooo

Jess: Ha, ha, ha I believe that.

Sam: There may have been a few late nights when I lost track of time.

Tata: Yea you Sam, besides making your dad and I argue about who isn't taking you to town during the highway construction.

Jess: I remember the tears and rage over those trees little sweethearts.

Sam: She always greeted me the same happy way in the morning with a cigarette and warm coffee. Opening the blinds and talking. She never ran out of good conversation and was always guiding and giving such good advice.

Sam: Oh yes and the tree that hit our house after I got hysterical that they forgot to pray for it. I cried when they cut the grass too I guess. Nana told me they are just giving mother earth a haircut.

Sam: When I got in trouble I'd go to my room crying, repeating I wanna go to Nanaaaaaas. And I'd stare at the trees and the wind and see the animals and people Lol. I'd try to remember where so I could tell Nana.

Jess: We all wanted Nana anytime we needed comfort. She was our safe place.

Jess: She was the only one who could get Boo to bathe those couple of years.

Sam: Ha Ha and how she spoiled us. She'd take us shopping with her and we'd come back with new barbies, and she'd say don't tell grandpa! Like he didn't see all three of us all stroll in with new toys and huge smiles on our faces.

Jess: HaHaHaHa yep.

Jess: OMG remember the commissary trips?

Sam: Oh my gosh. She would let me bathe in her trailer for hours LOL constantly heating water on the stove to rewarm it for me.

Jess: She held up my bra I was buying IN FRONT OF THE SOLDIERS "JESSY THIS ISN'T A BRA, IT'S A SQUIRREL CONDO" !!

Sam: Oh, her special mint tea when I was sick. Oh, and she would get so frustrated when she'd buy Lucky Charms and I'd only eat the mallows.

Jess: Yea the trailer baths, bagels and cream cheese, cinnamon toast and cocoa.

Sam: Yep and a freezer full of muffins and pies.

Sam: Her chicken in a basket-crackers and cheese.

Hess: Nilla wafers!.

Sam: My favorite was when she'd make chocolate banana cream pie.

Sam: Garage sales! Treasures. Just one more! LOL.

Jess: Does anyone else hear her in your head when you start to cry and she'd say "I know baby" she always said that when I'd be upset and her back tickles with her long nails.

Sam: Yes.

Sam: Brushing grandpa's hair.

Sam: Braiding it as he sat on the floor in front of her.

Sam: Or how he wore a pair of jeans with the SMALLEST hole and she would scold him for looking homeless!!

Sam: Always keeping him looking good.

Jess: There's the joke I'm the butt of.

Sam: Your holy pants drove her crazy!

Jess: "Jessy do I need to buy you new jeans honey"

Sam: Why would you spend money on jeans that are ruined?

Sam: We would pick tall grass on our walks for the horses too. I always thought that was fun.

Jess: Me too and that goat that bucked Cubby LOL.

Sam: There were two I'm certain she always put her faith in. Grandpa and the Creator. From life struggles to slick roads, and things always worked out.

Jess: 100% yes. She knew she could depend on them.

Sam: Gosh Cubby, Nana and Cody with the raspberries was a hoot, Cubby would get so mad and then you'd hear Nana "Cody!!"and he'd laugh and get that smile he'd get when he was being a turd.

Tata: She never ran out of love and patience for us.

Sam: It's true. And her humor was great. She always joked. Picked on Grandpa but boy he couldn't pick on us.

Tata: You Sam "my tongue fell out, it happens"

Sam: Our sensitive sally would get upset and she was quick to scold.

Tata: I can still hear "George leave the children alone"

Sam: Pow Wows will never be the same.

Char: It sure makes me smile reading about your Nana. She was a beautiful soul.

Sam: She was. There's no one memory or way to correctly describe the person she was.

Jess: She was the most beautiful soul. Thank you for being there for her.

Char: It was a blessing to help and have the opportunity to get to know her and love her. We just clicked and that was that. She was so easy to love.

Boo: At Nana's house we could always have "Nana breakfast" cookies, ice cream, cake, those sorts of things, us kids were so spoiled.

Boo: I remember when I was younger, about 6, I was sitting in the snow trying to make an igloo and Nana would be coming out trying to get me inside. She was worried I'd be getting cold. Finally, I went into Nana's and had a hot cup of cocoa. She always worried about us.

Boo: I remember Sam used to drive her crazy wearing her sweater around her waist in the middle of winter.

Boo: I remember going to Nana's house and became SO worried because the door was open, her shoes were in the house and nobody was home. Grandpa had taken her to the hospital. She had used an old razor on her leg, and it got infected.

Boo: Grandpa didn't know because Nana took the blame for me trying to burn their trailer down in Sutton. I was trying to be brave and light the heater, then threw the match in the trash and went out to play. Dad and Grandpa took the burning trash can out.

Boo: Nana couldn't make it to one of my school plays so I left her a voice recording on the answering machine of the song we sang. Grandpa still has that stupid tape.

Boo: I remember a story about Sam (I was only a baby) and a catfish named "Buddy" that Dad caught and she wouldn't let Dad and Grandpa eat it, so they
put it in the bathtub and it did die after all. Then she made them bury it… Poor Dad and Grandpa really wanted to eat that catfish. It was in the newspaper because it was so big.

Boo: When I was very young I'd find four leaf clovers and always run and give them to Nana so she could press them in books. I don't know how many I found but there were a lot of them. She would always give me a hug for them.

Boo: I remember the baby mini horse that the mom wouldn't feed and Nana had it in the cabin feeding it goat milk. She would sit in the recliner with it in her lap. It was named Spirit but they couldn't save it.

Boo: I remember Nana told me that Dobby was really bad when he farted. I was in the living room in the cabin and wow! I ran up the stairs yelling "Nana! you weren't kidding!" It was soooo bad from such a little dog!

Our Relationship

I've been asked by my children and grandchildren what is a solid one. I don't know if there are any "rules". I say no, as nothing is ever set in stone, for myself and Debi it was always a matter in total truth. That led us to trust in each other, safety in honest communication of all things. What we did or didn't like from the little things like leaving the lid off the toothpaste to intimate details, it was always better to know rather than guess or be misunderstood.

In arguments (which all people have) it was always resolved before bed regardless of how long it took. It was never left for the morning, this way we faced a new day with everything settled and forgotten, through agreement, compromise or respectful disagreement.

Understanding that the two of us were different in thought, views, and likes of many things. Two sides of the same coin between- love, truth, trust, respect for feelings, resolve and commitment to each other. We picked each other for life and that as with anything takes work, always a friend, partner, husband, wife and lover.

Never allow anything or anyone between us. Know that before there can be love there has to be respect seeing beyond the physical and to the action. Being there not just in the moment but always, doing what you say, walking your talk with each other always.

Being friends as well, finding fun and filling the days with laughter and just being the two people you are, never seeking to change each other.

We loved who we were and our differences. We had different personalities as everyone has. I have always been outgoing, she was more reserved. I appreciated those differences as did she. We supported each other in those differences.

The grass is never greener on the other side of the fence if you care for your grass, it will always be greener. So, I never worried about others nor did she about me, what we had we knew the worth of, much more than any fantasy. As the years passed, we of course changed and grew older physically but never lost the beauty and "handsomeness" we each fell in love with.

To me age made her more beautiful, and she seems to always glow. We kept "pinky secrets with our grandkids of course but nothing ever within our marriage or relationship with each other.

Nothing could ever be said about each other from others and taken as fact, we knew each other so well that we would finish each other's sentences. I don't know if this helps, I just know for us they worked, and it was always doing for the other before oneself, knowing the other felt the same way.

Our wish has always been that you, our children, would find that one person that completes you as we did.

We love you all dearly,
Grandpa

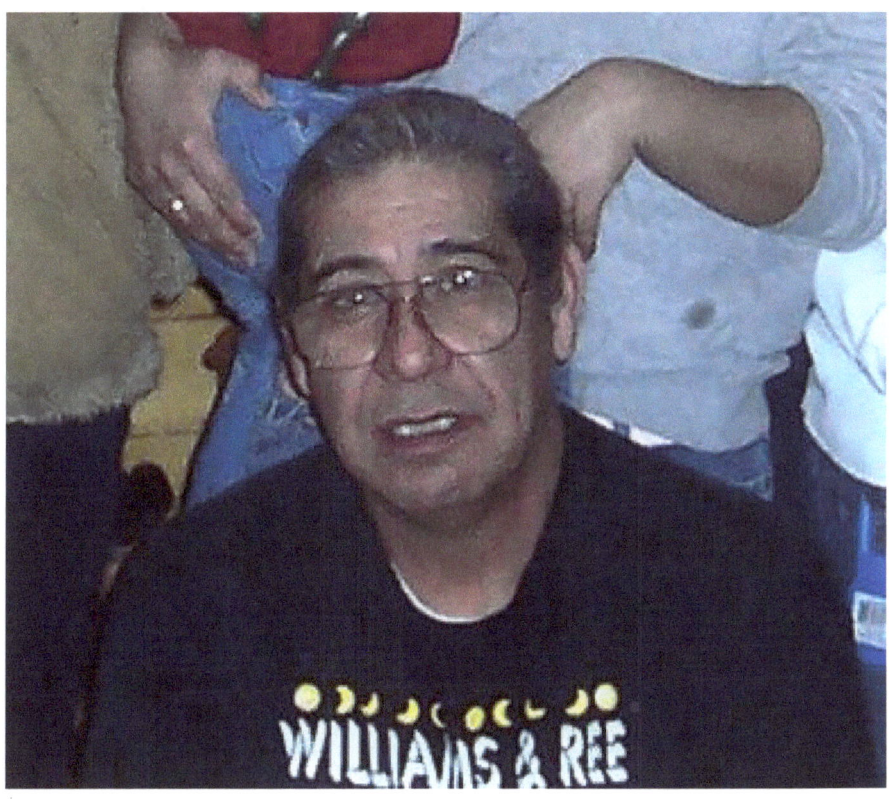

2nd row:
Rayan, Milli (Great Granddaughter), Sammy (Granddaughter), Wayne (Grandson), Travis, Mckenize, Cody (Grandson), Kellin (Great Grandson).

1st row:
Sadi (Great Granddaughter), Jessy and (Great Granddaughter) Emmy.

2nd row:
Shelby (B00) (Granddaughter), Koby (Grandson), Brandy.

1st row:
Nicky (Great Grandson), Jaxx (Great Grandson), Kyson (Great Grandson) and Shyanne (Great Granddaughter).

Seraphina (Great Granddaughter), Lucius (Great Grandson),
Steven, Reavyn (Granddaughter) and Glen (Son)

Chris (Son), Sammy (Granddaughter), Me (Grandpa),
Debi, Shelby (Granddaughter), Jaxx (Great-Grandson),
Brandy, Emmy (Great Granddaughter)

Mom, Missy and Debi

Debi and Dobby

Debi and Sammy (Granddaughter)

Debi, Koby (Grandson) and I

Debi and Sadie (Great Granddaughter)

Debi and Chockta

Oliver (Great Grandson), Rebbeca

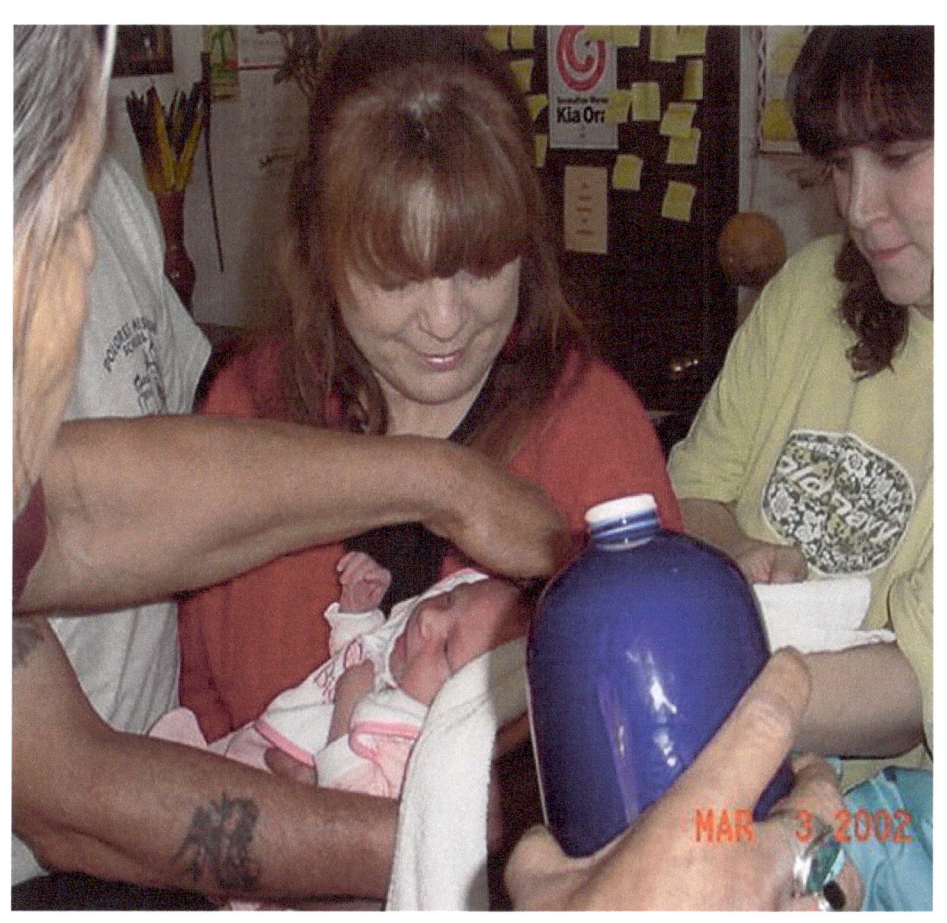

Me, Debi, Reavyn and Jane

Debi and Sammy (Great Granddaughter)

Darcy (Granddaughter), Aurora and Saphira (Great Granddaughters).

Myself, Debi and Chris (Son)

Debi and I

Family Tree

George - Vicky
George - Dee
George/Malin – Dee/David
Paxton- Oakland- Peyton

George – Debi

Missi	Glen	Chris
Missi/Phillip	Glen/Wendy	Chris/Brandy
Wayne Ezykiah	Darcy	Sammy/Rayn
Missi/Scott	Shayne, Aurora,	Emily
Jessey, Cody	Saphira	Chauncey
Jessy/Brain	Glen/Jane	Koby
Sadi	Reavyn	Shelby/David
Jessy/Travis	Raevyn/Steven	Jaxx, Shyanne
Milli	Seraphina, Lucius	Shelby/Doug
Cody/Rebeca		Nicky, Kaison
Oliver		
Cody/Mckenize		
Kellin, Riot, Nova		

KEY
Children/Spouse
Grandchildren
Great Grandchildren

When the day arrives that there are no more tomorrows for me...

I want my kids and grandkids to know and never forget that they were, are, and always will be deeply loved by me.